THE

APOSTASY:

AMERICA IS TURNING

AWAY FROM GOD

BY

A. J. FROST

ISBNs:

eBook: 9781966647843

Paperback: 9781966647850

Hardback: 9781966647867

Published by:

Authors Publishing House

178 Broadway, 3rd Floor, #1343

New York, NY 10001, USA

Main Line: (855) 624-0155

Email: support@authorspublishinghouse.com

Table of Contents

A Note from The Author

In this book, I endeavor to place events in a historical context by presenting the dynamics of a kingdom as it engages in the rise and possible fall of an empire. Each citizen is affected in some way by the community at large. *The Apostasy* offers renditions of these emerging kingdoms. I present material from the extensive research I have done, as well as my own ideas, for readers to consider.

Accounts of the culture and religion of the selected empires are the themes of this text. As the author, I suggest that an empire will fall if it is not built on a foundation supporting the Judeo-Christian God. All quotes from Scripture are taken from the *New International Version Bible*. Many definitions and explanations are taken from the *Britannica Encyclopedia*, *World Book Encyclopedia*, *Wikipedia*, and *New World Encyclopedia*. I have researched numerous books for data that give both support for and rejection of historical accounts.

A solution is offered in this book for the problem of apostasy in the "home of the free and land of the brave." My desire is that you will be enlightened and take on the determination to become a disciple of the Lord and that you will be committed to preventing the apostasy of America.

Acknowledgements

There are so many people who have helped me during my writing endeavors. I want to thank my grandson, Jeff Kersey, for being my personal I.T. advisor while he heaped words of encouragement on me when I most needed it. Thanks again, Jeff! I also want to thank my children, Jimmy, Don, and Karen, for their faithful encouragement.

I wish to thank Paul Ultis for locating books, reading them, and then loaning them to me to see if they offered useful information on the topics about which I am writing. I also want to thank my friends for their support and willingness to overlook the times I couldn't be present because I was busy working on this book. There are many staff members at Eagle's Trace Retirement Center in Houston, Texas, who have shown interest in and offered encouragement for my writing endeavors. I wish to give all of you a heartfelt "Thanks!"

Chapter One:
The Purpose for Writing This Book

"If God is your partner, make your plans big."

~Dwight L. Moody

The word *apostasy*, as found in the dictionary, is "the abandonment or renunciation of a religious or political belief." Is America turning away from God? I believe it is. It is my endeavor to share what I fear could bring this great nation to its demise – the fall of America.

We may think that we are not turning away from God. Some may say, in defense, "I believe in God." But does our behavior exemplify this profession of faith? Are we following God's dictates of how we should live? Do we make every effort to avoid the near occasion of sin?

The acceptance of many of the less-than-godly behaviors in our society does not follow the dictates of God's message to us. God gave Moses the tablets of the laws on the Ten Commandments, and Scripture states Jesus' words:

"I have not come to change the law, but to fulfill it."

How many of God's laws do we fail to observe? God has not changed since He anointed people to write down His Word; it is we who have changed.

Society no longer views it as unacceptable for couples to live together outside the bonds of marriage. Overindulgence in alcoholic beverages and the use of marijuana are now acceptable cultural behaviors. Acquiring wealth by less-than-godly methods so we can enjoy a better lifestyle seems to be socially acceptable. We indulge in calorie-laden cuisine loaded with chemicals that cause high blood pressure, heart disease, and cancer. We do not exercise regularly in order to keep the body in fit condition. We are not loving to our fellow man but often behave selfishly toward them.

These things may appear beneficial for us – to give us a better quality of life – but do they? Marijuana has been called the "gateway" to the use of stronger drugs. Probably marijuana and alcohol should both be in that category. While working on the adult psychology and drug unit of Charter Hospital, I was the psychotherapist for a male patient whose problems first started with a drinking problem that led to an addiction to heroin.

This patient was stimulated by the heroin. He became a workaholic. Because he worked such long hours, he had no time for his family. Being addicted to heroin creates many problems. Among these problems is the need for the addict to lie about his or her behavior. This person became irresponsible and could no longer hold a job or be relied on to be honest.

Many people in the world indulge in the use of drugs. The drug marijuana is widely used in our culture. The effects of using this drug produce a carefree, laid-back sense of "everything is well in my world." The drug enhances one's thoughts about being in control of circumstances, even when he or she isn't. The use of marijuana also interferes with healthy body functions such as appetite and sleep patterns.

How many crimes are committed in this country by individuals on alcohol or other drugs? How many faulty judgments are made by people using these drugs? How many vehicle accidents result from the use of drugs or by drunken drivers? How many people contract AIDS from using contaminated needles or having sex with an AIDS partner? This kind of behavior results in turning away from God.

Scripture shares the message with us that we are protected by God, our loving Father. But this promise is based on the premise that we must follow the advice given in His Holy Word. If we do not make every effort to follow God's will, we will reap the consequences. If we do not follow the will of God, we are definitely turning away from Him.

When America turns away from God, this has an impact on the world! Powerful empires produce leaders in world affairs. America has tremendous influence on world policies as well as the beliefs and religion of the cultures of the world. And because the media has instant access to reporting up-to-date happenings, citizens of the world share in the dynamics of this process.

My efforts are to give evidence in this book of the process that results in the fall of empires because they were not built on the foundation of God or were turning away from Him. The purpose of this book is to provide information, including ideas, research, and evidence, that supports the reason for my fear that we are turning away from God, who should be the cornerstone of the foundation of our nation. The many discussions I have generated on this topic, the outreach effort I have extended as Director of Gracegate Ministries International, and the prayers that come from every prayer warrior I can reach, are to pray for a Spiritual Awakening that will take the scales from our eyes and bring us to our knees in reverence to our Creator. As I prayed for a name for the ministry God has provided for me, "Gracegate" kept returning to my mind. This is the perfect name because His Son, Jesus, is the Gracegate through which we reach God.

In writing this book, I attempt to address the task God has put upon my heart – to warn my fellow Americans of the possible apostasy of "the land of the free and the home of the brave." I choose to use the expression "Spiritual Awakening" as the call for turning to God instead of "Spiritual Revival" because there are many who have never acknowledged belief in the Spiritual Sovereign that is God. These unbelievers cannot be revived but rather awakened. It is my hope and prayer that this book will shed some light on this endeavor.

As a basis for fear of the fall of the American Empire, I am offering a concise history of empires that at one time existed as leaders of the world only to later fall from that pinnacle because the foundation of that nation was not built on God. He lets us know when He is not pleased with our behavior. Starting at the beginning of time, according to the Judeo-Christian history of the Bible, I endeavor to present a brief look at the powerful position of the Ancient Empires. The Modern Empires are presented in the last half of the book.

The Ancient Empires consisted of Mesopotamia, the African Continent, the Empires of China, Japan, Akkadia, Assyria, Egypt, Babylon, Persia, Greece, the Early Roman Empire, the Australian Empire, and various other less familiar empires. We then move forward to later eras and get a glimpse of the struggle and severance of the relationship between the more recent Modern Empires and God. The Modern Empires include the German Empire of Bismarck, the Ottoman Empire, the Spanish Empire, the British Empire, the French Empire, the Russian Empire, the Austro-Hungarian Empire, and on to Hitler's Third Reich and America's position as a world leader. There are other empires about which this author did not write.

America's role in WWII elevated the position of this former British colony to a leadership position in world affairs. The old saying, "history repeats itself," comes to mind as we see commonalities and consequences in the rise and fall of empires. An attempt has been made in *The Apostasy* to offer the most accurate data that research provides. I am an avid reader and search many books on the subject about which I am writing. Books are always on my birthday and Christmas gift lists. Nothing pleases me more than to receive a good book as a gift. I live in a metropolitan area where "state-of-the-art" libraries are available to obtain books for research.

It is my hope that while reading *The Apostasy: America Is Turning Away from God*, the reader will be inspired to correct the negative factors pointed out by this author that could lead to the apostasy of this great land.

Chapter Two:
What Is the Standard for Right and Wrong?

"The Bible . . . but for it we could not know right from wrong."

~Abraham Lincoln

I have heard it said, "The truth is in the eye of the beholder." Added to this enigma is the statement made by Winston Churchill, "The victor writes about the outcome and the history of war." What can we accept as "the truth"? How are we to determine what is just or unjust? Who commits the first wrong in an offensive altercation?

The morés, customs, traditions, and civil laws determine the parameters for the behavior of citizens in our culture. There are universal "rules" that govern acceptable behaviors in society. There are behaviors that our courts deem illegal. As individuals, we have an internal barometer, God's Holy Spirit, which measures the gnawing of our conscience when we have committed a wrongdoing.

How does God reveal the way we are to live our lives? God anointed men to write scripture, which contains His awesome Word that gives detailed instructions on how we are to live. The mighty Word of God covers every dynamic of living. There is no subject left uncovered in God's Holy Writ

– the Bible. The Bible instructs us on what thoughts to think, the words we should say, and the way we are to act.

The Holy Bible is the chosen means of Judeo-Christians to reveal God's truth to the heirs of His Kingdom. It is the revelation of the power of the gospel – the "Good News" of Jesus Christ, the second person of the Holy Trinity. The Bible presents the history of the Israelites, God's chosen people, and the followers of Christ, who died on the cross for our sins. This Holy Book provides the parameters of the path to holiness, or as it is referred to in scripture, "The Way."

God's Holy Writ was written by anointed men. It is inspired. This author believes the Bible is inerrant and is a lesson plan for evangelizing. The Bible is the text to be used for pastoral sermons. It is the resource for Bible study classes.

It is from the Bible that we learn to lift up our Creator. We are to encourage others to study and follow the teachings of God's Holy Word. The Bible provides the guidelines for us to become a better person. It provides the means for each of us to become an effective disciple.

The great Pastoral Letters of Paul, who was chosen on the road to Damascus to become the "thirteenth apostle" and the one who wrote one-third of the New Testament, tell of salvation. Paul was imprisoned under Nero, the cruel and extravagant Roman Caesar who caused his own mother to be killed. Paul wrote many letters (epistles) to Timothy, his protégé. Paul had this to say about the Bible:

"All Scripture is God breathed and is useful for teaching, rebuking, correcting and training in righteousness, so that the man of God may be thoroughly equipped for every good work."

(II Timothy 3:16-17)

The apostles testified to the awesome power of God's Holy Word. It is authoritative. The truth can be found in the metaphors and parables of Scripture. It is the story of good and bad people as they struggle with life's challenges.

The Bible will confuse the most profound philosophers before it enlightens them. As we study this Book, we will be under the tutelage of God's Holy Spirit. It is the Spirit of God – the third person of the Holy Trinity – who interprets the profound words of Scripture as we read and study them. As we experience many great "ah-has," we will be filled with an incomparable peace that will sustain us through all trials and tribulations experienced in life.

God's Word is the armor that protects us when we are in harm's way. We should recall and recite Scripture as it is needed to sustain us in times of despair, danger, and hopelessness. When we are uncertain of which path to follow, we profit when we seek guidance from the Word of God. There is no emotion equal to the joy felt when we are living in the assurance of God's grace.

This can be likened to the final countdown before the launch of a spaceship. Many people are involved in the instructions and life-saving details that astronauts must learn in order to guide the spaceship on a successful path. Paul states that the man of God must be completely and thoroughly equipped. It is through man's relationship with God that he becomes thoroughly equipped to fulfill his purpose on earth.

The legal Code of Lipit-Ishtar and the Code of Hammurabi, King of Egypt, came into existence in early biblical times. These were dictates that set boundaries for civil law. Hammurabi was king of one of the Mesopotamian city-states. It was not until Moses was given the tablets that contained the "Ten Commandments" that laws addressing moral behavior came into existence.

It was during the wandering in the wilderness when Moses climbed the heights of Mt. Sinai and witnessed God as a burning bush that we received directions from God on the "Thou shall and shalt nots." Sinai was the highest mountain in the area. There were small, foot-size steps carved into the mountain that made the ascent less difficult. Perhaps Moses sought to be nearer to God.

This was such an important event in God's relationship with mankind that it was accompanied by smoke, earthquakes, and the blast of a trumpet.

"On the morning of the third day there was thunder and lightning, with a thick cloud over the mountain, and a very loud trumpet blast."

(Exodus 20:16)

The mountain was covered by smoke as if coming from a furnace. The whole mountain trembled.

The "Ten Commandments" hold the secret of happiness. Scripture contains many parables, metaphors, and stories concerning the "truth" of how we should live. God commands that we should "have no other God before him." If we follow this dictate, we shall have joy and peace within ourselves.

It is a sad thing that the "Ten Commandments" are often viewed as "restrictions" of our freedom. The truth is that these dictates are restrictions of a loving parent. The commandments given to Moses on Mount Sinai were given for our benefit. God is our Abba, and those rules were given as the act of a loving Father.

As has been said by others, "The Bible is God's love letter to man." It was written from God's own heart and, when considering the "Ten Commandments," written by His own hand. The "Ten Commandments" provide an explicit set of rules that will bring order and stability to our lives. This prevents chaos in our civil system, our family, and private matters.

God's commandments provide a frame of reference by which all people are to live. The tablets bearing the commandments provide God's truths, which include the criteria for determining right from wrong. They provide a system to determine just and unjust behaviors. God's commandments give us hope for the future.

God sets the standard for morality and the justification for right and wrong. God's righteousness reigns. God's attributes set the standard for the definition of righteousness. It is a sad thing that righteousness is not a quality we teach our youth to aspire to possess. Rather, they are encouraged to acquire an education that will bring them prestige and money.

It is a big issue for parents, educators, and counselors to advise the young to choose a vocation where they will be doing something they enjoy. What if they enjoy eating too much, taking another's possessions, sleeping with as many partners as they can, or projecting a reputation built on lies? The role models for success and living the good life hardly ever reflect on the righteousness of God. The righteousness of God is a forbidden topic for discussion in schools.

One of the themes of the New Testament is the righteousness of God. The gospels are described by Paul as the revelation of God's righteousness. The character of God, as revealed to us through His Son, is the model of what is right. We are to strive to become righteous.

To know the difference between right and wrong, it is necessary to strive to become righteous. God sent His Holy Spirit to groom us for righteousness. We are to grow in holiness or sanctification. We are called to stay in right relationship with God by obeying His laws and commandments.

We are not called to be self-righteous. We should always place ourselves in the biblical sense: "What would Jesus do?" WWJD is the question we need to ask ourselves when pursuing a chosen path. We should compare the questionable situations in our lives to biblical Scripture.

We are "in this world" but "not of it." We belong to the Kingdom of God. "God is the Sovereign and Christ wears the crown as king," was stated by John Adams, one of America's Founding Fathers. When we sense ourselves nearing the place of temptation, we need to send up a plea for righteousness, especially in a hostile environment.

We were made righteous by the sacrifice of Jesus on the cross at Calvary. We were also made victorious by the crucifixion of Christ. We are no longer slaves to sin! His destiny was the cross, His purpose was love, His reason was us.

We either have to attend church services, be enrolled in a church school, or a Bible study class to receive any information or guidance on our spiritual path. It hasn't always been this way. The Judeo-Christian Bible used in the first schools in America was once the book from which to teach the sons and daughters of the Founding Fathers. Now the Word of God has been removed from the classroom, books, lessons, and discussions.

The righteousness of God doesn't receive much attention in the secular world. Corporations do not have religious goals. Doing the "right" thing is rarely on the agenda of a board meeting. The commitment to do the right thing according to God has to be written on the tablet of the heart of a believer.

The words of prophecy, wisdom, reproach, and condemnation found in the Bible are the essentials for an empire to survive. When the citizenry of an empire renounces the Word of God, apostasy will result in the fall of that empire. This has been proven from the beginning of time. It is the fear of this author that the American nation is on the path of decline.

We should not let the Deceiver (Satan) tempt us to be unrighteous or break one of God's commandments. We should be prepared, with the wisdom from God's Holy Word, to fortify us on any occasion to choose the right thing to act upon. Pray daily for guidance from God to do His will. God will provide the strength to withstand any destructive behavior we encounter.

We need to listen to the still, small voice of the Holy Spirit for guidance in every aspect of our lives. The New International Version of the Bible states:

"But seek first his kingdom and righteousness, and all these things will be given to you as well."

(Matthew 6:33)

The New Living Translation of the Bible gives the following version of the same Scripture:

"Seek the kingdom of God above all else, and live righteously, and He will give you all you need."

The King James version of God's Holy Writ states the same chapter and verse as follows:

"But seek you first the Kingdom of God, and his righteousness, and all these things will be added unto you."

These Scriptures tell us to strive for a higher spiritual life and leave all else in the hands of the Father, and He will provide for us.

There is an exhibit in China that is called "The American God." This exhibit consists of a plaque containing a neatly framed dollar bill. That which holds the highest place in our lives is our god. In modern times, we seem to turn away from our Judeo-Christian faith and seek materialistic idols on which to spend our time and money.

There are a great many substitutes that are set up to replace the God of Abraham, Isaac, and Jacob. Some false teachers say that God is merely "the spirit of the community." Many people worship the pleasures found in life. Others worship reason, philosophy, or the knowledge of the intellect.

The first commandment states:

"You shall have no other Gods before me."

(Exodus 20:3)

It is because of God's love for us that He gave Moses the tablets that contained the commandments written by His own hand. The second commandment states that,

"You shall not make for yourself a carved image – any likeness of anything that is in heaven above, or that is in the earth beneath, or that is in the water under the earth; you shall not bow down to them or worship them."

(Exodus 20:4-5)

God is revealed to us in nature, and we were given written information about His attributes and supremacy in the Bible. God's Holy Spirit translates the Word of God as we read Scripture. We put our faith and trust in God's Holy Word. Those who have no faith wander in the wilderness without God's Glory Cloud to lead them.

The Glory Cloud is believed to be a physical manifestation of the presence of God.

"In all the travels of the Israelites, whenever the glory cloud lifted from above the tabernacle, they would set out; but if the cloud did not lift, they did not set out - until the day it lifted."

(Exodus 40:36)

As God's chosen people, the Israelites march through history being led by this Glory Cloud to the land promised them by the God of Abraham. Their saga is the "Manifest Destiny" of a chosen group of followers, both Jew and Gentile, who believe that they were elected by the supreme God of the universe to spread the good news of the gospels to the ends of the earth. God has displayed His glory in hundreds of ways throughout Scripture. The will of God is made known to us in Scripture. It is the will of God that we establish a relationship with Him that exhibits obedience to His commandments. As Jesus set the example, we are put on this earth to be servants to God and our fellow man.

The third commandment states that:

"You shall not take the name of the Lord God in vain."

(Exodus 20:7)

How many people violate this commandment every day? Jesus said:

"But I say to you that every idle word men may speak, they will give account of it on the day of judgment. For by your word, you will be justified, and by your words you will be condemned."

(Matthew 12:36-37)

"Remember the Sabbath Day, to keep it holy" is the fourth commandment of God.

(Exodus 20:8-11)

We are told that for six days we shall labor, but the seventh day is the day of the Lord. To obey this commandment, we are not to allow our children, our servants, our cattle, nor any stranger who is visiting us to do any labor on the Sabbath. God made this day as a day of rest, rejuvenation, and spiritual revival.

We are to honor God on the Sabbath. By observing this commandment, we recognize our Creator as being sovereign and worthy of the first claim to our time. No matter where we are or what we are doing, we should give God the glory and honor of being our Divine Progenitor. The Sabbath is the day set aside to rest and honor God.

In the book of Exodus, chapter 20, verse 12, God tells us:

"Honor your father and mother."

Although this is the fifth commandment, it is the first commandment that gives us a promise from God:

". . . that your days may be long and that it may be well with you in the land in which the Lord your God is giving you."

The sixth commandment states that, "You shall not murder." Restoration can be made for many of the wrongdoings we commit.

We cannot bring someone we have killed back to life. God gave us the ability to create life. We are commanded not to take life.

"You shall not commit adultery" is the seventh commandment written on the tablets brought down from Mt. Sinai by Moses to give to the Israelites.

(Exodus 20:14)

18

In defining the restrictions of this commandment, we need to understand the parameters of the definition. The dictionary defines adultery as "voluntary sexual intercourse between a married person and a person who is not his or her spouse." The following is found in the Bible in Leviticus 18:20,

"Do not have relations with your neighbor's wife and defile yourself with her."

This commandment is also found in Deuteronomy 22:22,

"If a man is found sleeping with another man's wife, both the man who slept with her and the woman must die."

The eighth commandment is,

"Thou shalt not steal." **(Exodus 20:15)**

This edict from God is just and easy to understand. No one desires to have what he has accumulated maliciously snatched away from him. This is a code of ethics in most cultures.

"You shall not bear false witness against your neighbor" is the next of the Ten Commandments.

(Exodus 20:16)

This includes gossiping and spreading rumors. At times, some of our "talk" may be based on correct information, but it is best not to spread hurtful information and stir up discord. The best thing to do when temptation lures you into this situation is to stop and pray for the people involved. The tenth and final commandment is,

19

"Thou shalt not covet."

(Exodus 20:17)

This is meant to not desire the wealth, good fortune, power, or prestige that others may have. We are to be content with the goods and the grace God has sent our way. If we are in need of something, take our supplications to the Lord. God promises to give us the desires of our heart if we abide by His will. My fiancé told me on one of our dates before marriage, "I am an ethical man." My response to him was, "But are you a moral man?"

Chapter Three:
The Torah, The Talmud, The Bible and The Koran

"If you don't know what you're living for, you haven't yet lived."

~Rabbi Noah Weinberg

In the Jewish faith, the Torah is a collection of the first five books of the Bible written by Moses or under his direction. Originally, many of the Jewish beliefs consisted of oral teachings and traditions. Many of these oral teachings did not make it into the original manuscripts but were studied for several hundred years by rabbis. The decision was made that these edicts and traditions needed to be written down.

In the Talmud, there are two divisions of learning—the Northern Israel and the Babylonian. The Torah and the Talmud form the basis for the Jewish faith. The Torah provides instruction on the law, while Talmud means "learning." The Talmud was written in 1342 BC, while the Torah was written in 1312 BC.

The Talmud is the main text and primary source of religious law in Jewish theology. The term Talmud refers to the collection of Jewish writings that serve as a guide for the daily lives of Jews. The Talmud is composed of two components, the Mishna and the Gemara. The Mishna is a collection of the detailed oral information on the Hebrew holy book, while the Gemara is a commentary and analysis.

The Bible, which is the holy book of the Christian faith, contains geographical and historical information about the migrations, battles, and lives of the Israelites and the followers of Christ. The Bible is the story of the men and women whose destiny was to portray the purpose that God left heaven to become the incarnate Messiah to be crucified on the cross for the sins of man. The fertile strip of land known as Canaan became the Holy Land that is inhabited and visited by Jews, Muslims, and Christians. The followers of Muhammed regard the Koran, or as it is also called, the Quran, as their holy book.

The Bible provides mankind with the purpose, truths, and relevance of existence. The first five books of the Old Testament, the Pentateuch, are also referred to as the "Five Scrolls of Moses." Moses received the tablets, which contained only ten commandments, but the Israelites added many additions to the first laws.

The first section of the Bible covers the stories of creation, from Adam to Noah. Next come the stories from Abraham to the times of Moses in Egypt and on to the exodus of the Israelites to their home in Canaan. There are accounts of the former prophets, the latter prophets, and the twelve minor prophets. These collective stories tell of Israel's monarchies from Canaan to the split of King Solomon's territory into the kingdoms of Israel and Judah. King Nebuchadnezzar of Babylon captured Jerusalem in 586 BC.

It is in the Bible that we learn that the Israelites vacillate between glorifying and worshipping Yahweh, or Elohim, as they called God, and forsaking Him to worship Baal or build a golden calf as an idol to worship. The geographical setting for Abraham, the father of the Hebrew (Israelite) nation, was in the land of Ur, which is in the Middle East.

Abraham, the patriarch of the Judeo-Christian Old Testament, was from Mesopotamia, which consists of what is now Iraq, Syria, Turkey, and part of Kuwait. It is in Scripture (text of the Holy Bible) that we learn of many ancient empires. Mesopotamia, Sumer, Akkadia, Babylon, and Assyria were political, cultural, and thriving centers of religious activity. The ancient empires also include the Egyptian Empire, the Greek or Hellenistic Empire, and the early Roman Empire.

The Koran, or Quran, is the holy text of the Islamic faith. It is believed by the followers of Islam to be a direct revelation from God through the angel Gabriel over a period of twenty-three years. It is regarded as one of the best works in Arabic literature. The Koran was written in the seventh century AD.

The Koran is organized into 114 chapters, which consist of individual verses. It presents themes and miracles based on the wisdom of Allah, the god of the Muslim faith. The followers of the Koran believe that Adam was the father of mankind. Ibraham, or Abraham, is the patriarch of the Koran. Jesus is considered a prophet in the Islamic faith.

The Koran promotes justice, peace, and restraint. It encourages believers to refrain from violence against one's brothers. Some modern critics say that the Koran promotes terrorism. Two of the requirements of the Muslim faith are to recite the Koran and to pray by using the words from this holy book. The revered prophet in the Islamic faith is Mohammed. Another requirement, if you follow the Islamic faith, is to make a yearly journey to Mecca, the place where Mohammed was said to have ascended to heaven.

Chapter Four:
The Shedim, Fallen Angels and Malevolent Spirits

"To return good for good is human.

To return evil for evil is brutal.

To return evil for good is diabolical.

To return good for evil is Divine."

~Royard

What if the source of the decline in the spiritual values of the world lies in the return of mysterious deities of the ancient entities referred to as the Shedim – "ancient gods and goddesses?" What if these deities have returned after a long absence and are presently hovering over us, casting negative influences on our behavior? There are leading theologians, authors of spiritual books, and believers who realize this could be the truth behind the apostasy of America. If fallen angels or pagan gods are attacking America, is it possible that they are also causing worldwide havoc?

If we are aware of their presence, will we make the necessary changes to prevent the demise of this great country and the nations that look to America for guidance? Since I am a believer in the Judeo-Christian faith, I always turn to God's Holy Word, the Bible, to search for answers to the solution I am seeking. I will search for the way God and Jesus guided the prophets, kings, apostles, disciples, and followers. This path should begin with prayer:

Dear Father in heaven,

> *Please fill my mind with Godly directions to write and address the concept of the apostasy of America and the possible effect such a transformation could have on the world. Fill me with your wisdom, Abba, to discern what is true in the historical accounts of the empires that have existed from the beginning of time and guide me as I finish the manuscript and get it published. Father, please put a burden on President Trump and make a place in his heart for your Holy Spirit to live as he becomes the leader of America.*

> *Amen*

Scripture states that one-third of the angels in heaven followed the angel Lucifer when he was cast to earth. Lucifer was called Satan after he was cast down to earth. The many references in Scripture devoted to this account of "The Fallen Angels" are so plentiful, they could make a study based on their own merit. Satan is the Lord of the Dark Kingdom, which consists of fallen angels.

Evil Principalities and Dark Powers are levels of demons and demonic activities. They are real, and their primary goal is to cause evil—to destroy, kill, and lure humans into committing wrongdoings or sin. They promote confusion and frustrate humans. This is done to retaliate against God for banishing them from the heavenly realm.

Satan was doomed and destined to be thrown into "The Lake of Fire" for eternity. These legions of demons make up "The Kingdom of Darkness." Demonic spirits can camouflage themselves and take on the appearance of man or beast to cause as much evil as possible. They work alone or join forces to conduct their atrocities.

"And no wonder, for Satan himself masquerades as an angel of light. It is not surprising then, if his servants masquerade as servants of righteousness."

(II Corinthians 11:14 - 15)

In yet another scripture, Jesus informs seventy-two disciples he had chosen to go ahead of Him and perform miracles in His name:

"The seventy-two returned with joy and said, Lord, even the demons submit to us in your name. . . I saw Satan fall like lightening from heaven. I have given you authority to trample on snakes and scorpions and overcome all the power of the enemy; nothing will harm you."

(Luke 10:17-19)

The power of these Principalities is not restricted to certain individuals or specific places. The power of the demons or evil spirits can be felt in entire cities or certain areas of the cities. Perhaps a Dark Shadow of Evil in the form of sexual immorality hovers over an area. There may be a high incidence of pornography, homosexuality, adultery, prostitution, sex trafficking, or other forms of sexual immorality in that area. The United States of America is one of the top offenders involved in human sexual trafficking in modern times.

Child abuse and molestation may be common in communities under the influence of the demons of Satan's Dominion. It would be very advantageous for these demons to infiltrate the legislatures of state capitals. Is it possible that these evil spirits are influencing our federal offices and the chambers of the legislature? Is it also possible that the media has been broached, or worse yet, is under the control of demons from the Underworld?

It is evident that some studios of the movie industry produce explicit pornographic films that reveal completely nude sexual activities. Magazines that influence the styles of couture display provocative fashions that are designed to arouse sexual attention. Pornographic materials flood the population in various forms—pictures and pamphlets included. Songs have been written that depict settings of violence, immoral, and irresponsible behavior.

Educational institutions have adopted slackened rules that have done away with "dress codes" and guidelines for acceptable behavior. This slackened standard allows tight-fitting apparel with low necklines, short dresses, pants that hug the derriére, and sheer apparel that often reveals the anatomy as much as a wet T-shirt. Murder is more prevalent in certain areas. Attacks, physical harm, and mass murders are committed—some by deranged people, some by relatives of the victim. At times the perpetrators are children too young to hold accountable for their monstrous behavior.

There are people who are possessed by certain evil spirits that can communicate with the dead. There are also people who are incited by evil spirits to spread malicious gossip that is so intense that the victim's character is assassinated. Some principalities may have a "gang mentality" operating over their region. The number and kinds of evil principalities are too numerous to identify all of them.

How do we identify the existence of evil spirits? How do we confront them? How do we extricate these destructive demoniacs? How do we prevent these demons from harming our children, loved ones, friends, and fellow men? What must we do to prevent these demons from infiltrating our governmental leaders and services?

When we turn to the awesome Word of God, we find out how Jesus and the disciples were instructed to drive the demons of the Underworld from this Worldly Kingdom. Scripture states that on this earth there are two kingdoms—"The Worldly Kingdom and The Kingdom of God." Believers belong to the Kingdom of God. God's Word is the double-edged sword that slays the dragons from the Dark Principalities. It is possible that the Sovereign of this Dark Power is none other than the Anti-Christ.

Most people who have attended Worship Service or Bible Study classes have heard the story of the inflictions placed on Job by Satan. He had seven sons and three daughters. Job was a righteous man who was greatly blessed by God. He owned seven thousand sheep, five hundred donkeys, three thousand camels, five hundred yoke of oxen, and a large number of servants.

The number seven signifies completeness. To have seven sons during Job's time was considered a great blessing to a father and his family. Job was truly blessed by the Lord. Great feasts were held in his house. In the Judeo-Christian faith, the father acts as priest of the family.

Satan responded to God after He told Satan that he could try to cause Job to sin:

"Have you not put a hedge around him and his household and everything he has? You have blessed the work of his hands, so that his flocks and herds are spread throughout the land. But stretch out your hand and strike everything he has, and he will surely curse you to your face."

(Job 1:10-1)

This account from Scripture reveals that Job was tested many times. His children, as well as his riches, were taken from him. Job was tormented, and boils covered his body. He questioned the reason for his birth. He was robbed of every blessing God had given him.

Many people placed blame on "something wrong" that Job had done and sought to give Job solace, advice, and consolation. He listened to each of them but kept his relationship with God foremost in the depths of his heart. Job forgave his friends for not believing in his innocence. He not only forgave them for their unkind behavior toward him, he prayed they would be blessed.

There are many great truths found in the Book of Job from the Bible. Among the words of wisdom we gain from this story of the suffering of an innocent man include:

(1) The defense of the justice of God in the face of evil.

(2) There exist individuals whose godliness is genuine.

(3) We sometimes suffer from the words of well-intended friends.

(4) The relationship between God and man is not exclusive and closed.

(5) Satan attempts to alienate man from his Creator.

(6) The suffering of man has meaning in God's plan of salvation and sanctification.

In the end of the story of Job, the Adversary, as Satan is often called, is silenced. Job's friends are silenced, and Job ceases his lamentations. The outcome of the struggle is that Job's wealth and blessings were restored. Once again, feasting and celebrations were enjoyed by Job, a righteous man of God.

We are faced with questions about Job's righteousness as well as our own. Are we righteous only because of the rewards we hope to receive from God? Is our godliness self-serving? There is probably some truth to these self-accusing concerns that conflict us. Have we accepted Christ as the Savior? Are we in right relationship with God? Do we recognize when we are being tempted by Satan and tested by God? How do we respond to the following Scripture?

"Man is born to trouble as surely as sparks fly upward."

(Job 5:1–7)

Will we make Job one more brick in the wall of defense of our faith?

We are a nation that proclaims to accept diversity of the many immigrants who come to our shores. After so many battles over social injustices fought in the past, the doors of American society were forced open to people of color, diverse origins, and religious histories. The reality is, it has taken many generations, conflicts, and struggles to reach the stage of progress we have achieved in this endeavor. And by the number of reversals of laws governing many of these issues, we are still struggling. "Roe vs. Wade" is an example of legislature being changed.

Our thinking seems to be, "We tried that idea; it did not work, so we are going to return it to the original position." How do we know what the right policies and legislative dictates should be? The answers are found in prayers and God's Holy Word. There is a right and a wrong way to address every issue found in daily living – shall we marry or just live together, should I have an abortion or put the baby up for adoption, do I take this grievance to court or work it out with my neighbor – there is a right and wrong way found in the Bible to address every aspect that is found in life.

The amount of money spent on drugs, including alcohol, psychological medications, and therapies, indicates that many of our citizens are less than pleased with having to make such important choices. Who do we choose to make decisions at a national level on issues as important as abortion? In the year 2016, Donald Trump was elected President of the United States of America. After studying the demographics of the voting constituents, we learned that President Trump was elected by the votes of Evangelical Christians. The Pew Research Center is based in Washington, D.C. This organization reports on demographic trends of Christian believers in the world.

Chapter Five:
What Makes an Empire?

"The Bible has been the Magna Carta of the poor and oppressed. The human race is not in the position to dispense of it."

~Thomas Huxley

In a historical context, kingdoms and empires are often used in the same sense. As the head of state, a kingdom is ruled by a king or queen and is referred to as a monarchy. An empire is ruled by an emperor or empress. An empire can have territories that are ruled by different kings. If the individual areas that make up the kingdoms are ruled by more than one king, it is called an oligarchy.

Kingdoms can grow into an empire. The emperor's authority surpasses that of a king. If the monarchy is a constitutional monarchy, its authority may be limited by a legislature or parliament. Differences between a kingdom and an empire can be between political structure, control, or the size of the area that is being governed.

An empire is described as consisting of a dominant central body of government and then lesser units of subordinate entities. The subordinate units are made up of villages, towns, cities, or large metropolitan areas consisting of diverse populations. History separates empires into two time frames – Ancient Empires and Modern Empires.

Another distinction for categorizing empires is that of separation between contiguous land-held territories that make up the empire and an empire that exists because of a powerful sea or air power of a ruling "home country," which may be in another part of the world. Examples of former empires are the Russian Empire and the Austro-Hungarian Empire. Examples of the latter category of empires are the once-reigning Spanish Empire with its powerful Armada and the British Empire, which once held the position of the largest empire in history, holding territories scattered throughout the world that were located great distances from Mother England.

Empires usually come into existence through conquest. The early group of colonies forming in America is an example of the growth and development of settlements, villages, towns, and ultimately city-states, metropolitans, country, nation, and empire. The United States of America became a nation of leadership in the world. Although it does not bear the title of "Empire," the United States of America has held a status of influence and power that suggests that it is an empire.

Historically, important settlements that become villages, cities, metropolitans, and eventually an empire have many characteristics in common. Geographic location plays an important role in the creation of an empire. Large or small, any settlement has a better opportunity to thrive and survive if it is located on a body of water that can transport people and goods. Water can be the source of creating power that operates the machines that produce the products needed for existence and pleasure. A tremendous quantity of water is necessary for consumption and domestic usages, which include commercial activities and sewage.

Another commonality that is necessary for the rise of an empire is the availability of communication between the separate groups of people located in each settlement as well as between the various settlements. Information can be communicated by various means such as smoke signals, carrier pigeons, messages floating in a bottle, Pony Express, telegraph, telephone, fiber optics, radio, and television. Communications are by land, sea, or air. Messages were carved on the walls of caves by the caveman. The early Egyptians used hieroglyphics and the cuneiform language to record significant events.

There are numerous stories, movies, educational curricula, and archaeological artifacts that provide data on the varied forms of communication. It is an important dynamic of any culture. The chosen form of government, rules, and laws, as well as customs and traditions, dictate the parameters for the behavior of the citizens of a future empire. The availability of resources for producing goods is a most important dynamic in the formation of an empire.

Provided services support how well the people survive. The quality of schools—from nursery school, kindergarten, through college and university, training programs, and trade unions—contributes to the growth of an empire. The availability of places to worship, honor, and glorify the Lord are foremost in the building of an empire. The seminaries and religious institutions have the responsibility to provide fellowship, to educate future pastors, leaders, and laypeople who will teach our young people about salvation, how to become mature Christians, and the ways of the Lord and Savior, Jesus Christ.

A thriving empire is built on a spiritual foundation that contains the cornerstone of the Lord. Israel is an anomaly that stands on the Holy Ground of three religious faiths – Judaism, Islam, and Christianity. This author writes spiritual books based on the Judeo-Christian faith. God is the Author, and I am the co-author. It is my endeavor to do,

"My Utmost for His Highest."

~Oswald Chambers

In the following chapters, I will present a brief synopsis of the history of the rise and fall of many of the leading empires, the people, and the culture that make up the empires in existence at that time. There were other empires that existed, sometimes simultaneously, at times during a different era. I make use of an author's discretion and present the most notable empires remembered. The selected empires appear in a somewhat chronological order.

The task that I am pursuing is not an easy endeavor. Please indulge my efforts and forgive my inadequacies. I am advanced in years and tire too easily. As I feel called by God to plead with my fellow man, when writing this book to abide by His will, I am certain He will keep me on this earth long enough to comply with the task.

It is beneficial to this writing to offer explanations and also share some of my opinions. I believe that there is a lot of the author in the story he or she is telling. One of my beliefs has to do with the labeling of the time eras. Until fairly recently, our time tables used the expression BC to designate "Before Christ" and AD as "Anno Domini," which means "After Christ." This labeling of eras was used worldwide.

In more recent times, the connotation BC was changed to BCE, meaning "Before the Common Era." I view this as part of a plan to take Christ out of usage in our faith-based culture. So, I do not use the BCE expression. I also do not use the expression "Xmas" to designate Christmas. I will not "take Christ" out of Christmas!

Chapter Six:
The Timetable We Use to Study the Rise and Fall of Empires?

"There is a time for everything, and a season for every activity under heaven . . ."

(Ecclesiastes 3:1)

Studying how time has been ascertained since the beginning of written historical accounts is helpful in understanding the dynamics of the rise and fall of empires. Hopefully, the more knowledgeable we become about our spiritual history, the more benevolent, merciful, patient, and caring we become toward people, animals, the land, and our world. Our Creator separated light from darkness and water from the firmament. He gave us patterns of nature and seasons as guidelines to be useful in our existence.

The account found in the Book of Genesis tells us about God's timetable surrounding the events of creation. Although it is written in Scripture that seven days was the time allotted to create the world, there was no time designated for the length of a day.

"In the beginning God created the heavens and the earth. Now the earth was formless and empty, darkness was over the surface of the deep, and the Spirit of God was hovering over the waters."

(Genesis I:2)

On the first day, God created light and darkness, night and day, morning and evening. On the second day, God created the expanse He called "sky," and below the sky were the firmaments and the waters. Vegetation was created on the third day. God created seed-bearing plants and the trees. Among these trees was the "Tree of Knowledge of Good and Evil."

It was on the fourth day that God placed a great light in the heavens to determine day and a lesser light to distinguish night from day. He also created carefully arranged groups of stars. He set them to shine on the earth and to govern the day and the night.

"And God saw that it was good."

(Genesis 1:18)

Living creatures, great and small, were placed in the waters. Birds flew in the sky, and God blessed them. And this was the fifth day of creation. And all that God created was good.

Wild animals and living creatures that move on the ground were created on the sixth day. Our Lord created each type of creature "according to its kind." He created livestock according to their kind and wildlife according to their kind. He created the creatures that moved along the ground according to their kind.

On the sixth day, God said, "Let us make man in our image, in our likeness" (Genesis 1:26). He declared that man would rule over the sea. Man would also rule over the birds in the air, over the livestock, and over all the creatures that move along the ground. Man gave names to all the creatures God had created.

God was finished with His creation. He rested on the seventh day. He blessed the seventh day and made it holy. God saw all that He had made and declared it to be good. He was pleased.

Man was formed from the dust of the ground. God breathed into the nostrils of man and gave him life. Man did not have to work the land to grow food to eat. There were various types of fruit to provide sustenance. Streams of water came from the earth to irrigate the land.

God saw that man had no helper, so He caused man to fall into a deep sleep. He then took a rib from man and created a helpmate to be his companion. Man said:

"This is now bone of my bones and flesh of my flesh; She shall be called woman for she was taken out of man."

(Genesis 1:23)

And so, God established a time frame, a reference to help mankind in the endeavor to plot designated segments of space that proved to be necessary when meetings, descriptions of intervals, and predictions were made between people. Artifacts from ancient empires have been found that reveal sophisticated means of predicting and keeping a record of time. The digits of man's hand, rocks, beads, sticks, or marks made by a stylus have been useful devices to assist in marking time. God graced man with reason, imagination, and a thumb and forefinger to grasp to make tools to help record timely historical events.

When time is the subject of conversation, we need to make sure we are considering segments of the same moment of existence. What would we do without time schedules? We tell others that we will meet them at a designated period (time). At what hour, day, week, or month do we refer when arranging an appointment? The world would be chaotic without a consensus of time.

Before there was a calendar, the earliest time segments of civilization were drawn or carved as characters on the walls of caves and later in hieroglyphics and cuneiform figures in the pyramids. These were drawings and inscriptions of the motions of celestial bodies. The ancient astrologers tracked the sun, moon, and stars. The Mayan pyramids, Stonehenge Monument, artifacts from Egyptian ruins, and the Aberdeen Pits in Scotland reveal the ability to predict "time" in ancient civilizations.

Through the centuries, discoveries of events in nature that correlated with celestial bodies were made. Examples of these include the rising and setting pattern of the sun, the tide rising and receding with the moon, the menses in women, the changes in the shapes of the moon, and many other occurrences. Perhaps the people who devised the first calendar were motivated by food. It was necessary for our early ancestors to track seasonal growth rates in crops in order to plant and harvest.

They also had to know the time of migration seasons and paths of animals in order to hunt and kill prey for food. The sun is predictable and can be depended on to follow a regular cycle. It is trustworthy to follow the same pattern year after year. The cycle of the moon is dependable and is correlated with the behavior of nature.

During 2013 in Scotland, archaeologists uncovered what is believed to be the oldest lunar calendar. This discovery consists of a series of twelve large pits dug by people from the Mesolithic period. These specifically shaped pits appear to portray the different phases of the moon. The pits were aligned to the midwinter solstice.

This arrangement would assist the hunter-gatherers of the area to keep accurate data of the passing of seasons and the cycle of the moon. These groups were early nomadic wanderers that roamed the areas in search of food and shelter. This discovery in Aberdeen, Scotland, pre-dates by several thousand years the Bronze Age monuments found in Mesopotamia. It is important to understand that cultural information on past civilizations depends upon what archaeologists find and how the findings are interpreted.

New findings supersede past information as new data is uncovered. Artifacts of history depend on an endless search for new findings. During the Bronze Age, over 5,000 years ago, the Sumerians in the Tigris-Euphrates valley developed a calendar. This calendar was based on four natural phenomena: (1) the unit of the day, which was based on the sunrise and sunset due to the rotation of the earth; (2) the position of the sun during sunrise and sunset; (3) the change in the elevation of the sun above the horizon throughout the year; (4) the lunar month, which was correlated to the moon. There were always twelve months in a year.

The Stonehenge Monument in Wiltshire, England, has no written data explaining its origin or purpose, but the arrangement of the structures provides definite information on celestial, time-related phenomena. The time period of the origin of this configuration is approximately 3000 or 2935 BC. The Stonehenge Monument is aligned to the sun. There are burial mounds located within three miles of Stonehenge.

It is suggested by archaeologists, historians, and theologians that the burial grounds are possibly those of ancient priests who were perhaps in charge of the Stonehenge happenings. These important happenings would be under the care of someone in the hierarchy of the emperor or king. Gold, precious and semi-precious stones, grain, and animal sacrifices were made to the god of the times around these structures. The areas have been looted throughout history, and anything of value that could be carried away was taken.

Religion played an important role in ancient civilizations. Emperors and kings were supposed to be strong leaders. Priests were held in high esteem. Often leaders were advised by priests, councils of men, and magicians. The queen, consorts, and prophetesses also "had the king's ear."

In the year 2510 BC, the Egyptians came up with their version of a calendar. This calendar was based on the moon's cycles. They included a star named Sirius to aid in counting time. The Egyptians added five more days than the Sumerians to their year.

King Romulus, in 738 BC, came up with a Roman calendar. This calendar started in March, and each month had an even number of days. This method of calculation caused the seasons to be out of sync every year. There were 354 lunar days designated by King Romulus' calendar.

During the twenty-first century BC, King Shulgi of Babylon united previous calendars into the Umma calendar, which became the basis for the Babylonian calendar. The Umma calendar also had twelve months in a year and a thirteenth month every four years. Every seventh day of this Babylonian calendar was considered a day of rest. On each day of rest, Babylonian officials made offerings to a different god.

The next calendar mentioned in history is the Julian Calendar, which was introduced by Julius Caesar, the emperor of Rome. Caesar sought astronomer Sosigenes and several mathematicians to develop this calendar. It was the most used calendar of the Roman Empire and the Western world for over 1,600 years. The Julian Calendar was used until Pope Gregory introduced the calendar, which is now in use in most of the world.

With the Gregorian Calendar, Easter occurs on the Sunday following the ecclesiastical full moon that falls on or after March 21. This calendar is based on the movement of the earth around the sun. It consists of 365 days in a year, but as on the Julian Calendar, a leap day is added every four years. On this calendar, the 365-day year is divided into twelve months or fifty-two weeks, seven-day weeks, and 28–31 days in a month. Although Pope Gregory did not design the calendar, it was given his name.

Chapter Seven:
The Mesopotamian Empire - Man's First Home

"God saw all that he had made and it was very good."

(Genesis 1:31)

From the earliest rendition of the historical Hebrew and Greek sacred texts, man's first home was located in Mesopotamia. Mesopotamia was an early biblical region. This geographical location is present-day Turkey, Iraq, Syria, and parts of Kuwait. The first kingdom God created was perfect. It was designed by our Creator to be a paradise.

The history of the origin of man is given to us in the book of "Genesis" found in the Old Testament. The first Hebrew phrase in the Old Testament contains the word *"Bereshith,"* which is translated to: *"In the beginning."* Theologians state that God is "all powerful – omnipotent, all knowing – omniscient, and with us at all times – omnipresent." Having faith, as Believers in Christ, we know that God has the power to do all things. After all, He created the world. God desired to have fellowship with the people of the first kingdom—Adam, the first man, and Eve, the helpmate God created from a rib taken from the body of Adam.

The first kingdom was called the "Garden of Eden," and man was the caretaker of God's Garden and all the creatures that lived there. God let Adam name all the animals. Trees were planted that were beautiful and provided tasty food for nourishment. God walked, talked, and had fellowship with Adam and the woman Adam named Eve.

The serpent God created was deviant and crafty and convinced the woman, Eve, to eat from the Tree of Life, which had been forbidden to do so by God. The serpent said to Eve in Genesis 3:4.

"You surely will not die."

She in turn gave some of the fruit to her husband, who readily accepted it. The place that once brought joy and fellowship with God became a place of fear for its inhabitants.

Adam and Eve were created by design of God to enjoy a relationship with Him. Their purpose in life was to stay in right relationship with God. They wore no garments of clothing, and food was provided for them without having to work. They were to live forever without experiencing death. The Garden of Eden was truly Paradise.

After tasting the forbidden fruit from the Tree of Life, Adam and Eve realized they were naked. When God came for His usual stroll through the Garden with them, ashamedly, they hid from Him. They took leaves from the fig tree and made clothing to cover their nakedness. Because the serpent was the one who enticed Adam and Eve to partake of the forbidden fruit,

God placed a curse on the serpent, on Eve, and then on Adam because he ate the fruit that Eve offered him even though it was forbidden. God also cursed the ground, and from that time on, favorable vegetation brought forth would be accompanied by unwanted weeds, thorns, and thistles. The Lord informed Adam,

"By the sweat of your brow you will eat your food until you will return to the ground, since from it you were taken; for dust you are and to dust you will return."

(Genesis 3:19)

Because Eve disobeyed God and offered the forbidden fruit to Adam, God informed her of the future position women would hold:

"I will greatly increase your pains in childbearing; with pain you will give birth to children. Your desire will be for your husband, and he will rule over you."

(Genesis 3:16)

God banished Adam and Eve from the Garden of Eden. He placed Cherubim and a flaming sword to flash to and fro, to guard the entrance to the garden. Cherubim are beings that were created by God to perform divine duties upon the earth. The Cherubim are depicted as winged bulls or lions with human heads.

Flavius Josephus, a Jewish scholar and historian, was hired to write the historical account of the Israelites. He stated that the number of Adam's children was thirty-three sons and twenty-three daughters. Josephus was a hero of the military, a scholar, and a Jewish priest who was born in Jerusalem in 37 AD. It is from the history written by Josephus that we gain much of our information on the Israelites.

The Father of Church History was Eusebius Pamphilus. He was a bishop, theologian, and historian. He wrote on the discrepancies of the Gospels. Eusebius' most famous work was *Ecclesiastical History*. This is the first mentioning (outside of the Bible) of the twelve followers of Christ.

One of the descendants of Adam was Noah. Because mankind was corrupt and had only evil thoughts, God chose to destroy the world He had created by a great flood. Because Noah was a righteous man, God provided specific details for him to build an Ark. Along with Noah, his wife, three sons, and their families were to board the Ark. Noah was then instructed by the Lord to gather two (a male and a female) of all creatures upon the earth and load them aboard the Ark.

Noah, his family, and the creatures placed aboard the Ark according to the instructions of God were spared, while everyone else drowned in the flood. God made a covenant (a formal alliance) with Noah whereby He promised never again to send a great deluge of water to destroy the world. God chose the rainbow in the storm clouds as a sign of this unconditional Divine promise.

There are three types of covenants found in the *Bible,*

1. Royal Grant – issued by the emperor, king or sovereign leader.
2. Parity – a declaration of friendship or respect for each other's interests.
3. Suzerain Vassal - one that is an agreement between the chief of state and a subordinate subject.

Noah was the new father, following Adam, of the human race. The sons who survived the Flood were Shem, Ham, and Japheth. Ham was the father of Canaan. The name Canaan was later declared in biblical history to be the name of the Promised Land given by God to the Israelite Nation.

The descendants of Noah were to be God's heirs who were scattered over the earth. These descendants became the twelve tribes of Israel. Many of the famous people and locations referred to in Scripture bear the names of these descendants of Noah. The Judeo-Christian Bible is the history of these people. One of the accounts revealed in Scripture is that of the occasion when Ham discovered his father lying naked in his tent in an inebriated condition. Ham then went outside and informed his two brothers of witnessing his father's nakedness. The brothers placed a covering across their shoulders and then walked in backward so they were unable to gaze upon their father's nakedness. They approached the bed and covered him.

When he awoke, Noah found out that his youngest son, Ham, had not covered him after discovering that he was naked. Noah cursed the descendants of Ham for not covering his nakedness. Canaan, Ham's oldest son, bore the brunt of the curse. Canaan and his descendants became the slaves of Japheth and Shem.

The account from the Bible of the descendants of Ham, Shem, and Japheth is a "Table of Nations" that existed in Mesopotamia after the Great Flood. There were fourteen nations that came from Japheth, thirty from Ham, and twenty-six from Shem. The total makes up seventy nations.

Another patriarch of the Old Testament was Abram. He was among the descendants of Sem. Abram's name was changed by God to Abraham. Terah, who was Abraham's father, was from Ur, which was located in Mesopotamia. Terah worshipped idols of polytheistic gods. Abraham was married to Sarai, whose name was changed by God to Sarah, who was also born in Ur. Sarah was Abraham's half-sister.

Abraham had a nephew named Lot. When Abraham traveled to reach Canaan—the Promised Land—he took his nephew Lot with him. Lot settled in an area not too far from his uncle, Abraham. God often visited with Abraham. The following account tells what happened to the place where Lot lived.

On one of these visits, the Lord informed Abraham of the immoral sexual perversion being practiced in Sodom and Gomorrah. Men were having sex with other men. God did not approve of this behavior. This was an abomination to the Lord!

The Lord said,

"The outcry against Sodom and Gomorrah is great and their sin so grievous that I will go down and see if what they have done is as bad as the outcry that has reached me . . ."

(Genesis 18:20–32)

It was then that Abraham was bold and negotiated with the Lord concerning the number of righteous men to be found. This example, found in Scripture, brings up the question, "Can we negotiate with God?" Abraham asked God:

"What if only ten righteous men can be found?"

God replied, "For the sake of ten, I will not destroy it." Two angels went to Sodom that evening, and Lot persuaded them to stay at his home where he fed them. But before they went to bed, the men from Sodom surrounded the house and called out to Lot:

"Where are the men that came to you tonight? Bring them out to us so that we can have sex with them."

(Genesis 19:5)

The men of Sodom were homosexual. The act of anal sex comes from this account in Scripture and is called "sodomy." It was then that Lot replied:

"No, my friends, don't do this wicked thing. Look, I have two daughters who have never slept with a man. Let me bring them out to you and you can do what you like with them. But don't do anything to these men, for they have come under the protection of my roof."

(Genesis 19:8)

The men would not listen to Lot and attempted to break into his house. But the men in the house pulled Lot back into the dwelling. It was then that the men attempting to break in were struck with blindness and could not find the door. Two angels were sent from God to inform Lot they were going to destroy Sodom and Gomorrah.

The angels said,

"The outcry to the Lord against its people is so great that He has sent us to destroy it."

(Genesis 19:13)

When dawn arrived, the angels urged Lot and his family to leave. Lot hesitated, and the angels grabbed his hands and urged him, along with his family, out of town.

"The Lord rained down burning Sulphur on Sodom and Gomorrah – from the Lord out of the heavens."

(Genesis 19:23)

Lot's wife looked back and was turned into a pillar of salt. It is surely true that God works in mysterious ways! There are people who say this rendering is unjust because Lot offered his daughters to the men of Sodom and Gomorrah. The way I interpret the Words of Scripture is that anointed men reported the events the way they happened. They did not say that Lot was right in his choice of behavior or circumstances.

If Lot knew what was going on in Sodom and Gomorrah, why did he choose to live close by? Are we guilty of similar wrongdoings? At times, do we allow ourselves to come too near the occasions of sin? For one, I am certainly guilty. Too often, my choices carry me close to situations where sin runs rampant.

For many years, Abraham and Sarah were without children. As was the custom found in early sacred texts, Sarah's handmaiden, Hagar, was given to Abraham, and a son, Ishmael, was born to them. Several years later, Sarah miraculously conceived a child, and a son, Isaac, was born. It is believed by many that the descendants of Abraham and Hagar make up the inhabitants of the Arab nations, which are Muslim. The descendants of Abraham and Sarah make up the Semitic or Jewish population of the world. Many believers in the Judeo-Christian faith believe that the birth of Ishmael marks the beginning of the Islam faith.

In Islam, Ishmael, who is thought to be the progenitor of Mohammed, is the son of Ibrahim (Abraham). A covenant was made between God and Abraham, whereby God made a pledge to Abraham and all his descendants that He would be the God of the Hebrew Nation. Isaac, the son of Abraham and Sarah, had twin sons, Esau and Jacob. Since he was born minutes before Jacob, Esau would be entitled to the birthright – the Bekorah.

But Isaac's wife, Rebekah, who favored Jacob, dressed him in Esau's coat and thus deceived her almost blind husband into blessing Jacob. Esau was furious when he discovered the deception, and Rebekah sent Jacob to Haran for safety. During the trip, Jacob dreamed of a ladder extending upward into heaven. At the top stood God, who reaffirmed His covenant with Jacob's grandfather and his descendants.

"The land on which you lie I will give to you and to your offspring."

(Genesis 28:13)

Jacob built an altar upon the land, anointed it with oil, and called it Bethel – "the house of God." Once in Haran, Jacob worked for his uncle Laban, and through his uncle's deception, married both of Laban's daughters, Leah and beautiful Rachel. Leah bore Jacob six sons and a daughter. The sons were Reuben, Simeon, Levi, Judah, Issachar, and Zebulun – and a daughter, Dinah. Rachel gave birth to a boy named Joseph and later another son named Benjamin. Jacob's lesser wife or concubine, Bilhah, bore Jacob two sons – Dan and Naphtali. Zilpah gave Jacob Gad and Asher. These became the twelve tribes of Israel. Jacob later adopted sons Manasseh and Ephraim.

On his way returning home to Canaan, Jacob met with a stranger who was perhaps an angel or God Himself. They wrestled all night, and after the struggle, the stranger told Jacob from then on forward, his name would be known as Israel – "the one who prevails with God." Some theologians believe that the name has significance and means that just as Jacob, or Israel, struggled with God, so would the nation of Israel struggle for centuries with obedience to God.

At this time, all the people in the world spoke the same language. It was during an attempt to build a tower in Babylon that would reach heaven that God caused the builders to speak different languages. This is why we have the word "babel" in our language. Speaking different languages would make it more difficult to work together to build a structure that would reach the place where God resides, surrounded by heavenly angels.

The Babylonians also built beautiful hanging gardens that were one of the most outstanding features of all time. But their foundation was flawed. They did not have a foundation built on the solid rock of the Lord. The foundation of the Babylonians was built on false gods, worldly interests, and riches.

Empires may rise to great status, but they will surely fall if the foundation is built on any but the foundation of God. God uses mysterious means to bring about the plans and purpose for His heirs. We are the heirs of God's kingdom. He is an awesome God, but He expects obedience to His Word.

Chapter Eight:
The Empire of India

"You must be the change you wish to see in the world."

~Mahatma Gandhi

India, one of the oldest civilizations in existence, also has one of the highest mountain ranges in the world — the Himalayas. This mountain range separates the subcontinent plains of India from the Tibetan plateau. There are more than 100 peaks in the Himalayas that exceed elevations of 23,600 feet above sea level. The name Himalaya comes from Sanskrit (a classical Indo-Aryan language), which translates to "snow" and "abode."

There are many rare species of flora and fauna that can be found only in this region of the world. India has the greatest landmass in South Asia. It shares borders with Pakistan on the northwest. Nepal and China are on the north, and Bangladesh to the east. The Indian Ocean is on the southern border.

Genetic scientists reveal that anatomically modern humans first arrived on the Indian subcontinent between 73,000 and 55,000 years ago. In almost every culture in the ancient world, early man manifested belief in a Higher Power. Rituals were performed regarding this Higher Power. Adherence to these rituals became necessary to be a part of the community.

The beliefs, later called "religions," developed into dogma and liturgy. I have made it known of my belief in the Judeo-Christian Faith. I cannot say that other faiths do not contain God's truths. I can only say that it is my belief that God is awesome and we can never understand all of His ways. Each individual is uniquely made by God. I truly believe that there is no one who knows everything about God. I listen to what others say and then I watch what they do. I am not to judge them. I am told in Judeo-Christian Scripture to love my fellow man. I am also told in Scripture,

"For in the same way you judge others, you will be judged, and with the measure you use, it will be measured to you."

(Matthew 7:2)

I know that I do not always do the right thing, but I make a great effort to follow the teachings of the Savior, Jesus Christ.

As I searched the history books, I found that what is known about the earliest history of India was found in archaeological discoveries. The first known culture in this part of Asia is called the "Indus Valley Civilization," which existed from 2500–1500 BC. During 321–185 BC, the Mauryan Dynasty united most of India. The "Vedic" period of Indo-Aryan culture emerged during the time period between 1500–500 BC.

The Rigveda is a term in Sanskrit that means "praise" and "knowledge." The Rigveda hymns are an ancient Indian collection taken from Vedic Sanskrit and passed down among the families of India. The Veda is one of four sacred canonical texts used in original worship services from ancient India. Three of the four Vedas were lost over the years.

The Sakalya Shakha is the only Veda that survived and is still in use. An early Aryan civilization, which consisted of people who spoke a common language with people in Iran and Europe, occupied north and north-central India. These people spread south and eastward. The communities adopted an ancient form of social hierarchy of individuals.

This system was referred to as a "caste system." Early evidence of the caste system appeared in the Vedas more than two thousand years ago. The caste system depends on the concept of family ties and is referred to as "Jati," which means birth — referring to the biological family. Each family member is expected to follow the family's set of rules for behavior.

This set of rules of behavior addresses such matters as kinship, diet, and occupation. Jatis are assigned to one of four caste clusters called the Varnas. A person is expected to marry someone within the same Jati. It is expected that kinsmen will observe the Jati tradition.

In 250 BC, the "Asoka" culture started the practice of Buddhism in India. From 320–500 AD, the Gupta Empire made its debut with the "Classical Age of India." The Delhi Sultanates ruled India from 1206–1526 AD. The Mughal Empire dominated most of India between 1526 and 1857 AD. European trade resulted in the establishment of British India (British Raj).

The British Raj, in 1947, began the colonization rule of India and impacted India in many ways. There were heavy British taxes imposed on the landlords as well as the peasants. Cash crops led to commercialism and at times resulted in famine. Destruction of Indian crafts and promotion of British wares affected the Indian economy.

The introduction of equality, human rights, and liberty inspired hope and freedom. Freedom brought about human rights and legal reforms that outlawed "sati," the burning of the widow on her husband's pyre, and female infanticide. There were negative outcomes as well as positive improvements during the colonization by the British. There was a railroad network system built under British rule that facilitated the transport of people as well as goods throughout the country.

There were over 1,500 different dialects spoken in ancient India. The present constitution in India recognizes twenty-two languages. In modern India, over 14% of the people speak English. Hinduism is the synthesis of various cultures and traditions.

In Porbandar, India, Mohandas Karamchand Gandhi was born on October 2, 1869. Gandhi's mother was very religious. The family followed the beliefs of the Hindu god Vishnu. Along with the beliefs of Vishnu, Gandhi's mother taught him the fundamentals of Jainism, which advocates nonviolence and the belief that everything in the world is eternal.

After completing earlier school studies, Gandhi enrolled in Samaldas College in India. Following this, Mohandas Gandhi left in 1888 to attend law school in London. While in London, Gandhi met playwright George Bernard Shaw and social reformer Annie Besant. He was also introduced to the Bible and the Bhagavad Gita.

The Bhagavad Gita is translated to mean the "Song of God." This book is the text that is studied and followed by those who practice Hinduism. The text describes a dialogue between Krishna and Hindu Prince Arjuna, an Avatar (reincarnation) of Vishnu. This is a sacred text of Hinduism. It addresses the ideal behavior for every aspect of life.

After becoming an attorney, Gandhi left for a job offer at an Indian law firm in South Africa. While in South Africa, Gandhi was subjected to racial discrimination. He was imprisoned several times for resistance and noncooperation. He defended those who suffered physical abuse, and job and housing discrimination. A law was passed in South Africa that required all Indians to register before they would be given permission to live there.

Gandhi advised those discriminated against, when they refused to register, to continue fighting with passive resistance. The law was abolished. Gandhi aroused attention from people in South Africa, London, and Calcutta. It was at this time that Mohandas Karamchand was given the title "Mahatma," which means "Great Soul." Mahatma Gandhi returned to India.

After returning to India, Gandhi continued to fight racism. He campaigned for self-rule. Gandhi launched a noncooperation effort against Britain. He initiated the spinning of khaddar, the Indian cotton, to make textile goods at home. Gandhi encouraged the people of India to boycott British goods, courts, and government. Gandhi continued to fight against discrimination. He attempted to unite Muslim and Hindu. On March 12, 1930, Mahatma Gandhi began a protest march from Ahmedabad to the coastal town of Dandi on the Arabian Sea. He was accompanied originally by 78 followers but picked up people from the villages they marched through along the way. This march was a nonviolent protest of tax resistance against the British salt monopoly. The Indians owned the land adjacent to the sea where the salt was obtained.

The British expected the people to pay for the process involved in attaining the salt while Britain benefited from the profits involved. This was viewed as an injustice by the citizens of India, and Mahatma Gandhi urged the people to protest. A march to the sea was planned. Thousands backed Gandhi in this protest.

They marched for twenty-four days. The protestors walked for 240 miles to their destination. This was a direct act waged against the British rule of India. Gandhi continued his struggle against the British Raj by hunger strikes and ignoring British rules of authority.

After a great political and social struggle, India won its independence from Britain on August 15, 1947. There were one hundred sixty-five million Indians killed during the British rule. Jawaharlal Nehru was an associate and follower of Mahatma Gandhi. He was India's first Prime Minister after independence.In 1930, a separate homeland concept for Muslims was introduced. In 1940, Mohammed Ali Jinnah urged for Pakistan, a separate Indian state for the Muslims of India. In 1946, Hindus and Muslims clashed over the formation of an interim government. Mohammed Ali Jinnah was a barrister and politician. Jinnah also served as the leader of the All-India Muslim League from 1913 until the inception of Pakistan. He was considered the founder of Pakistan. He then served as the country's first Governor-General. He held this position until his death.

On January 30, 1948, the assassination of Mohandas Karamchand Gandhi by a Hindu nationalist, Nathuram Godse, occurred at about 5:15 P.M. Gandhi traveled with his two granddaughters from his home to a summer pagoda where he made his evening devotions. It had been a pleasant trip.

The assassin greeted Gandhi as though he were glad to see him, then shot him at close range. He fired three shots. Gandhi was hit in the upper thigh, abdomen, and chest. As he died, Gandhi whispered, *"He Ram, He Ram — My God, My God."* The assassination set terrified Muslims against fundamental Hindus. Throngs of people left their homes to worship at Birla House. Troops were sent to maintain order. Prime Minister Jawaharlal gave a radio address and proclaimed "a day of mourning" to pay tribute to the man India loved.

The national capital of India is New Delhi, which was built south of the historic hub of Old Delhi. There are many ethnic groups and several languages found in this empire. The population exceeds over a billion inhabitants. The government of India is described as a Sovereign, Socialist, Democratic Republic.

Beautiful sites to visit in India include the Taj Mahal in Agra, the Golden Temple in Amritsar, and the Mecca Masjid Mosque in Hyderabad. Other interesting places are the Golden City in Jaisalmer, the Amer Fort in Jaipur, Periyar National Park in Madurai, and Agra Fort near the Taj Mahal. Kolkata (Calcutta) and Darjeeling are also interesting cities to visit. Martin Luther King, a Nobel Peace Prize recipient, had this to say about India: *"To other countries, I may go as a tourist, but to India, I come as a pilgrim."*

Chapter Nine:
The Empire of Africa

"It feels like God visits everywhere else, but lives in Africa."

~Will Smith

Africa is the second largest continent in the world, following Asia. It covers one-fifth of the land surface of the earth. Africa is bounded on the west by the Atlantic Ocean. The Mediterranean Sea is to the north of Africa. On the eastern side, Africa is bounded by the Indian Ocean. On the southern border is the Atlantic Ocean.

The name Africa likely comes from the Greek word "Aphrike," which translates to "without cold." Africa was joined to Asia by the Sinai Peninsula until the Suez Canal was built. There are fifty-four countries in Africa. Two levels of government operate this huge, mysterious land—the indigenous government, which pertains to local groups, and the national government, which pertains to the government of the nation-states.

In 1974, a collection of several hundred pieces of fossilized bone was discovered in Ethiopia, a landlocked country in East Africa. The assemblage of these bones provided evidence indicating that the fossilized bones were those of a bipedal young adult female over three million years old. Scientists have compared the information gathered in this archaeological find to other information gathered on the development of mankind. Because of the risk of damage to the bones, casts were made to display this archaeological discovery around the world.

On the night of the discovery of the fossils, the expedition group was dancing and singing around the bones while listening to the Beatles' song "Lucy in the Sky with Diamonds." The female skeleton was named "Lucy" by Pamela Alderman, a member of the group. This fossil discovery evoked worldwide interest. The discovery was one of the most important events of the time.

The U.S. tour of these fossilized bones, entitled "Lucy's Legacy," was on exhibition from 2007 to 2013. The original fossils were eventually returned to the country in Africa where they were found. They were placed in a museum. Part of the proceeds from the tour was used to modernize Ethiopia's museum.

Fossil remains of *Homo erectus* date back to Africa as the origin of man. So, we ask, "Was man's first home in Mesopotamia, India, China, or perhaps Africa?" Many sources of evidence indicate the Mideast as man's first home. There has been speculation that Noah's Ark has been spotted on Mt. Ararat in Turkey, near the borders of Armenia and Iran.

Greeks, Phoenicians, and migrants from Europe and Western Asia established colonies in Africa. The North African coast was colonized by the Phoenicians. Carthage, which means "new city," was a Phoenician colony founded in 814 BC. Gothic Vandals established a colony in the fifth century, which fell to the Byzantines.

This land eventually fell to the Arabs in the seventh century, which resulted in the Arabic language and Islam religion having an influence in Africa. The history of African colonization includes ancient Greeks, Romans, and Malayans settling in Africa. In the late 1400s, Europeans began arriving in Africa and setting up trading posts. The Dutch established a colony in 1652 in what is now Cape Town, Africa.

In the late 1800s and early 1900s, European powers dominated many parts of Africa. The principal powers in the modern colonization of Africa were Britain, France, Germany, Portugal, Spain, and Italy. The language used in government affairs is the language of the region that is in power. The natives speak the language of their tribe. There are ideological, tribal, and geographical differences among the people in Africa, which lead to conflicts.

The people are placed into three groups—bands, tribes, and kingdoms. The economies of the bands are based on hunting and gathering. This includes the Bushmen, the Kalahari, and the foragers of the central African forests. Each band consists of kinsmen who are governed by the traditional rules of the leader. Africa has existed a long time under this system.

Africa covers 6% of the earth's total surface area. It is divided equally by the equator. There are an estimated 3,000 tribes in Africa. Native languages or colonial languages are spoken. There are many different dialects. Swahili is the common language spoken by many.

A wide range of resources can be found on this continent. Fossil fuel sources are plentiful. An abundance of mineral deposits can be found. Stories tell of King Solomon's diamond mines. Animals for food are plentiful.

Colonial Africa is well depicted in the memoirs of Karen Blixen, a wealthy Danish royal who bought a large tract of land in Africa during the colonial era in the early 1900s. Karen Blixen's coffee plantation was at the foothills of the Ngong Mountains outside of Nairobi, in what is now Kenya. Baroness Karen Blixen's memories are told in her book *Out of Africa.* Most of the natives on Karen Blixen's plantation were from the Kikuyu Tribe.

There were natives living nearby who were from other tribes, such as the Somali, who also lived in the area. Baroness Blixen ran a school for the adult natives and children. Each morning, she provided medical care for anyone who required it. A young teenage native boy appeared one morning with sores spread over his legs.

Karen sent him to the nearby hospital for treatment. The boy returned later, healed from the sores and filled with joy at the newly found Christian faith he acquired while in the hospital. He became chief of plantation activities. There are hints in Karen Blixen's story of an intimate relationship with

Denys Finch-Hatton, a British hunter in Africa. Robert Redford and Meryl Streep starred in the Hollywood movie named *Out of Africa* after Karen Blixen's book.

Africa is home to such exotic animals as lions, leopards, cheetahs, hyenas, elephants, hippos, and rhinos. Reptiles such as crocodiles, pythons, and cobras are also found in Africa. A concept called "factory farming," which maximizes output while minimizing cost, is a growing industry in Africa. Animals pay the greatest price in this industry.

The United Nations Food and Agriculture Organization (FAO) suggests that the consumption of beef will increase by 200% by 2050. Poultry consumption will increase by 211%, and the consumption of pork by 200%. There is considerable support for the industry of factory farming. The negative factors often go unchallenged despite the drawbacks.

There are certainly some species of animals in Africa that are not found elsewhere in the world. Two species of rhinoceros are found in Africa, and three species of rhinos are found in Asia. Tigers are not found in Africa but in the wilds of Russia, China, and South Asia.

Tales of human beings stolen from or sold into slavery by their fellow African tribesmen are documented by officials. Slavery in Africa has a long and sordid history. The continent of Africa is among the areas of contemporary slavery, even though the situation is not technically called "slavery." The Ashanti Empire in Africa has been involved in perpetual warfare over the lucrative export of slaves. Child soldiers, forced marriages, and human trafficking exist in modern Africa.

Each of the fifty-four countries in Africa has different languages, unique beliefs, and customs. African religions are diverse. Christianity, along with Islam, is widely practiced in Africa. Most of the African religions support the belief in one creator—God. African ancestors are considered guardians of moral order. Masks play an important role in religious practices. Circumcision and removal of the clitoris are part of African religious rituals.

Chapter Ten:
The Empire of China – The Land of Cathay

"The journey of a thousand miles begins with the first step."

~Old Chinese Proverb

In early times, Chinese communities united to form villages, which grew into states and continued growing until they reached the status of kingdoms. Extended family members formed the concept referred to as a dynasty. Each dynasty had leaders who became powerful in political and governmental affairs. The most powerful person in the most powerful dynasty was chosen to be emperor of China.

The "Mandate of Heaven" was introduced by the Zhou Dynasty. This dynasty existed during the 1046–256 BC era. The most powerful man from the most powerful dynasty was supposedly sanctioned in heaven to become Emperor. Empress Wu Zetian was the only female to ever become Empress and rule over China.

The earliest written record of the existence of China dates back to 1600 BC. The people united under the rule of Qin Shi Huang into an empire in 221 BC. Some of the earliest dynasties were the Xia, the Shang, and the

Zhou. These people settled along the Yellow River and the Yangtze River basin.

Ancient Chinese history spans several thousand years. Writing appears to have developed in the early eras of Chinese history. Unity, fracture, strife, and prosperity were experienced at different times in the history of China.

"The Hundred Schools of Thought" were ideas and philosophies that appeared during the Zhou Dynasty.

These included the philosophies of Confucianism, Daoism, Mohism, and Legalism. Information concerning the military history of China was also discovered. These philosophies offered many suggestions on the way to live to the inhabitants of China. Articles of music, pithy statements, and eulogies, as well as writings about geography, were discovered as artifacts of history.

Articles written by Sima Qian from the Han Dynasty were found in excavated tombs. Large encyclopedias were written in China during different eras. Such writings were discovered from the eras of the Song Dynasty, Ming Dynasty, and Qing Dynasty. Written materials revealed information on Buddhism, which was a religion from India that was adopted by many Chinese.

Philosophy and religion were interchangeable concepts in ancient China. Confucianism, Taoism, and Buddhism were the three main religions of ancient China. Religion in ancient China was diverse. At times, the people practiced a combination of Buddhism and Taoism along with a Confucian worldview. This formed a view called Chinese Folk Religion.

The 1,100-mile-long Grand Canal in China, constructed as the world's longest waterway, links Hangzhou with the capital, Beijing. Rivers located in North and East China form links connected to other rivers, resulting in a most important water-borne transport infrastructure between North and South China. Construction of the waterway probably began as early as the fifth century BC. It is divided into six main subsections.

The Grand Canal passes through eight of China's twenty-three provinces. It knitted China together for fourteen centuries. The transported goods are diversified. Sometimes the shipment is grain, sometimes soldiers, and at times it is people with ideas to present to the people living in the heartland and the political capitals of the North.

This waterway is a crucial conduit of cultural communication. It provides clean, potable water to the North. It has lock-gates to regulate the water levels. The Grand Canal has been admired by engineers, civic developers, and visitors throughout history. It has been designated as a UNESCO World Heritage Site.

The acronym UNESCO stands for United Nations Educational, Scientific and Cultural Organization. The organization promotes peace, social justice, human rights, and international security. This organization also promotes independent media and freedom of the press. UNESCO rebuilds schools, libraries, and museums that have been damaged or destroyed. The organization gets funding from voluntary contributions, member states, and fundraising programs.

Another of China's exceptional wonders is "The Great Wall." This wall consists of a series of fortifications protecting the border of China. Long stretches of mountains and semi-desert terrain made original construction of the wall difficult. The wall was constructed to protect China's northern border. Some of the materials used in the construction of the wall were compacted dirt, stone, and man-made brick.

Some areas of land near the wall are brackish, so grass and crops do not grow in those areas. The wall is not continuous but is composed of segments. It is approximately 13,200 miles long, fifteen feet wide, and twenty-six feet high. Different dynasties made contributions to the extension of the wall, while other dynasties repaired the existing wall.

The wall has watchtowers, troop barracks, garrison stations, and signaling devices. It has been called by many names in the past. The structure is a form of protection from nomadic people led by warlords from the Eurasian Steppes. Construction of the wall possibly started as early as the seventh century BC. The best sections of the wall are those built during the Ming Dynasty.

As well as offering defense, there are controls that regulate trade and the number of people entering and leaving the area. The Wall also offers a means to transport goods from one place to another. There are many tourists who travel great distances to see "The Great Wall of China." This phenomenon was placed on UNESCO's list of World Heritage Sites in December 1987.

Another important phenomenon in the history of China is that of "The Silk Road." The "Silk Road" was a network of trade routes which began in the second century BC and was active until the middle of the fifteenth century.

This trade route got its name from the silk cloth that was first produced in China and then carried to European lands far away. The road was four thousand miles long. Many items, such as animals, spices, ideas, and diseases, were exchanged along the Silk Road between different parts of the world.

Another great event that contributed to China's prosperity was the relationship of Marco Polo, the infamous merchant from Venice. Polo wanted to travel East, so he joined his father and uncle on their return trip in 1271 for China. The entourage reached Emperor Kublai Khan's court in 1275. Kahn was the first emperor of China who was not born in that country. He was born in Mongolia. Marco Polo lived in Kahn's court and became his envoy representative for seventeen years.

Silk was highly valued in Marco Polo's country. Since he was a merchant, silk was a valuable commodity to be carried by convoys sent back to Italy.

Roads had to be built and maintained to ensure that silk, gold, silver, spices, and other commodities would make it from China to Italy and merchants who lived in other countries.

Emperor Kahn requested that one hundred missionaries be sent to China from Rome to teach the Chinese about Christianity. The Pope sent only two missionaries, and along the way, they were ambushed and killed. Perhaps if the Pope had sent one hundred Christian missionaries, the Chinese would not be atheists today.

The imperial palace complex, located in the Forbidden City, in the center of Beijing, China, has been declared to be worth seventy billion dollars. This makes this World Heritage Site the most valuable real estate in the world. It was the residence of twenty-four Chinese emperors from 1420 to 1912. The Forbidden City's construction took fourteen years to build. The Imperial Palace is one of the most visited sites in the world. It once housed the ruler's concubines.

The history of the world is full of "if only's" and "what if's." God is the Creator. He is the ultimate Architect, Law Maker, Legal Enforcer, Benefactor, and Heir apparent to everything in existence. Everything belongs to God—from the beginning until the end of time.

Another historical happening that had a significant impact on Chinese history was "The Opium Wars." These wars were fought over the trade rights of China and those of the conflicting powers in the West. The Qing Dynasty was in power during the time of the First Opium War. The Opium Wars were fought by China as an attempt to suppress the illegal trade of opium.

In the beginning, opium resin was ingested to give the user a "high." Opium is obtained from the unripe seeds of the opium poppy plant. Later, the drug was mixed with tobacco. This produced a more powerful "high." It was also at this time that tea from China became a favorite beverage of the Western world. "Tea time" also became a ritual enjoyed by British society.

Many smokers of opium-laced tobacco became addicted. It was reported that ninety percent of young adult men along China's East Coast were users of opium. This led to social and economic problems that disrupted the lives of the Chinese. There were people, both Chinese and from other countries, who illegally profited from the disruption caused by the use of opium. The disruptive and harmful effects of opium use caused great concern for Chinese governmental officials.

The British had been illegally exporting opium from India to China since the 1700s. The British East India Company was growing opium plants in India and selling them to private merchants who then transported the opium to China, where they sold it to Chinese smugglers. By 1797, the British East India Company was selling approximately 4,000 chests of opium a year, which weighed seventy kilograms each, to Chinese merchants.

Several emperors issued edicts at four different times—1729, 1799, 1814, and 1831—making the use of opium illegal. American merchants entered the trading through the smuggling of opium from Turkey into China. The trade of this formidable plant increased from 4,000 chests to 30,000 chests per year. This was a profitable (millions of dollars per year), but illegal venture that reduced the welfare of the citizens of China.

In an attempt to thwart the disruption caused by the use of opium, Chinese officials destroyed British-owned stockpiles of the plant. In retaliation, naval warships were sent to China by England's Queen Victoria. This was the beginning of the First Opium War.

China was not a formidable opponent as it was strategically and technologically unmatched to Britain. Britain had a fleet of steam-powered, armored gunboats. China could not compete with the advantages of the British Empire. The First Opium War ended, and an agreement was made between Great Britain and China.

The 1842 Treaty of Nanjing documented China's defeat and listed a series of humbling provisions, which included an indemnity and granting British access to the island of Hong Kong. The Qing Court also agreed to allow British access to five other ports for trade. This ended the existing policy of non-engagement with the West. China's political power had been weakened. This war began on September 4, 1839, and ended in August 1842.

The Second Opium War began on March 3, 1856. This conflict was between the British and French allies against China. During this conflict, China's elaborate Summer Palace was looted and burned beyond use. European powers gained domination over the powers of China. They gained control of the Russian-Chinese border and destroyed China's military.

The Second Opium War was also known as the Arrow War and the Anglo-French War with China. This war forced China to legalize opium and cede territories. The situation in China led to China being the battleground for Euro-American imperialist powers. The Qianlong Emperor made the following statement: *"Our celestial empire possesses all things in abundance and lacks no product within its borders. There is, therefore no need to import the manufacture of barbarians in exchange for our own products."*

After this statement was made by the Emperor, the British increased the quantities of opium flowing into China from India. By 1839, the Emperor of China decided to put an end to the British smuggling of opium into China. He appointed Lin Zexu governor of Canton, an important city on China's Pearl River. Zexu confiscated opium pipes and chests of opium worth millions of dollars and placed them in trenches. Chinese governmental officials then covered the opium items with lye and drenched the objects with water to destroy them.

British smugglers were arrested, tried in Chinese courts, and found guilty of smuggling. They were sent back to Britain but were set free upon arrival.

After this occurred several times, British trade with China was suspended.

The Second Opium War in China ended on October 18, 1860.

China is often referred to as "the cradle of civilization." This has been supported by scientific data suggesting the concept of the origin of man. In 1921, a tooth was discovered in a Zhoukoudian cave in China. Other fossils were found upon further excavation.

The initial discovery created a dialog between Eastern and Western science experts. Western scientific journals advocated that Africa was "the birthplace of civilization." Chinese scientists provided data that suggested that the "birthplace of civilization" was actually in China. These scientists suggested that China was the origin of Homo erectus in the lineage of man. This site yielded fossils from forty incomplete skeletons.

These fossils were carefully assembled to form the remains of anatomically modern humans. One such arrangement of a male skeleton was given the title "Peking Man." Further discoveries produced sophisticated tools used for different tasks. Evidence indicates that "Peking Man" used fire for lighting, heating, and cooking. This archeological site has been designated to become a UNESCO World Heritage Site.

Modern China has undergone a cultural revolution. The People's Republic of China, established in 1949 under Mao Zedong, projected that all Chinese literature should reflect cultural and class-standing attitudes and values. This made texts, school books, publications, and speeches subservient to Chinese politics. The idea was to increase the consciousness of a New Society.

This idea became the guideline for the Chinese people. These beliefs follow the tenets of Socialism. Special privileges to individuals are frowned upon. In the last two decades, competition over purchases of products between China and the U.S. has caused great tension between the two nations.

Beijing is developing measures to revive global governance institutions, policies, and norms. This measure is designed to make them more compatible with China's authoritarian political model. China belongs to an organization called the B.R.I.C. Alliance (Brazil, Russia, India, and China). This organization promotes a plan to replace the base of the monetary system in the U.S. (dollar) and Great Britain (pound) with cryptocurrency by 2050.

Modern China's religions include folk religions along with Buddhism, Islam, and Christianity. The People's Republic of China officially promotes an atheistic view. Some Chinese people protest the strict controls of religion in their country and have held demonstrations against the rigid restrictions and controls mandated by law. One such demonstration resulted in the deaths of many Chinese dissidents.

In June of 1989, students held a six-week protest in Tiananmen Square in Beijing, the capital of China. The protest was to mourn the death of liberal Communist Party leader Hu Yaobang. The students also protested the slow pace of promised reform. Although the number of deaths is debated, some reporters and Western diplomats stated that thousands were massacred during this protest. As many as ten thousand students were arrested. It was reported that tanks ran over students.

Chapter Eleven:
The Japanese Empire

"We learn little from victory but much from defeat."

~An Old Japanese Proverb

Japan consists of a string of islands stretching 1,500 miles through the North Pacific. More than four-fifths of the rugged landscape is made up of mountains. Mt. Fuji, at an elevation of 12,388 feet, is Japan's highest mountain. Due to abundant rainfall, Japan has a variety of crops.

Early inhabitants were tribes of hunter-gatherers characterized as pit-dwellers. Clay vessels have been found from 1500 BC. The Chinese Book of Han contains the first written information on Japan. Early considerations mandated that all land be distributed equally among cultivators. A household record was kept for taxation purposes.

Although Japan has a rich diversity of religious beliefs and practices, they coexist while influencing each other. The oldest form of religion developed from observing nature. The people of ancient times believed that animals and plants possess divine power. They believed that the rocks, trees, rivers, animals, places, and people possess "kami" – a sacred or divine essence.

This folk philosophy grew into a practice of worship called "the way of the gods." The Japanese word for this expression is "Shinto." In the sixth century, Buddhism and Confucianism were brought into Japan from other places. The people often co-mingle religion and philosophy. This results in a form of Japanese Folk Religion.

There are shrines for the Shinto believers to attend worship services, and there are temples for the Buddhists to attend. The Shinto believers often erect altars in their homes for reflection and worship. The followers of Shinto have many gods in their religion. Buddha was not a god but a revered leader-philosopher who found peace through enlightenment and rebirth. Confucianism focuses on the relationship between humanity and heaven as presented by the founding philosopher, Confucius, during the "The Hundred Schools of Thought" era in China.

An Imperial Court and other governmental systems that were similar to Chinese systems were established in Japan by powerful leaders. The feudal era of Japan was characterized by a class of warriors called the "Samurai." After an era of many military conflicts, a new power emerged called the "Shogun." Battles, defeats, and conquests became the pattern for centuries.

During the 16th century, Portuguese traders and Jesuit missionaries reached Japan. This began Japan's first relationship with the West. Oda Nobunaga used European technology to conquer other warlords. After Nobunaga's death, his successor attempted two unsuccessful invasions of Korea in 1592 and 1597.

Japan developed an isolated, "closed country" policy for the next two centuries. This was known as the Edo Period. Japan operated within its own boundaries. The country was capable of surviving without outside trade or resources.

Matthew Perry was sent by the U.S. Navy to convince Japan to open up to the outside world. This expedition resulted in the Convention of Kanagawa in March 1854. Japan adopted Western political, judicial, and military institutions and ideology. As a result of this endeavor, Japan emerged as the most highly developed nation in Asia. The Meiji Restoration movement of 1868 abolished a strict class structure and created a democratic system that paved the way for prosperity for the next century.

Following victories in the 1894–1895 war with China and the Russo-Japanese War in 1904 and 1905, Japan gained control of Taiwan, Korea, and the southern half of Sakhalin. Sakhalin is an island in northeast Asia off the coast of Russia. It is the largest island in Russia. The island has belonged to Russia and Japan at different times.

In the early 1900s, Japan began a period of expansionism. The 1920s witnessed a time of lawlessness. This was followed by the great Tokyo earthquake in 1923. Over 140,000 people were killed. One and a half million people were left homeless.

Japan resigned from the League of Nations in 1933. In 1936, Japan signed a pact with Nazi Germany agreeing to invade China. In 1940, Japan invaded French Indochina. The U.S. placed an oil embargo on Japan.

On December 6, 1941, Japanese military forces attacked U.S.-occupied Pearl Harbor, as well as British Hong Kong. WWII lasted until the U.S. dropped an atomic bomb on Hiroshima on August 6, 1945. The official surrender of Japan was on September 2, 1945. Japan's Emperor Hirohito and many military leaders were tried for war crimes.

After the war, allied occupation of Japan was under the leadership of General Douglas MacArthur. Political, economic, and social reforms were enacted. The Japanese military was dismantled. The occupation undertook the reformation of society, hoping to ensure that Japan would never again be a threat to world peace.

The Japanese people began to realize their full potential. Japanese leaders realized that power lay in industrial capabilities. Education, housing, economic issues, public health, recreation, and cultural values were addressed. Modern Japan has reached the point of being free, peaceful, prosperous, and democratic without losing treasured traditions.

Chapter Twelve:
The Empires of North and South Korea

"Do not attempt to teach a fish how to swim."

~Old Korean Proverb

Korea is a peninsula in northeast Asia. Historical records reveal that the peninsula was settled by Tungustic-speaking people who migrated from Manchuria and Siberia. These migrants settled along the coasts and river valleys. The early settlers lived in dugouts built slightly above the ground. The shelters were huddled together in groups.

By 4,000 BC, Stone Age farmers from individual tribes were living on the peninsula. By 1,000 BC, these farmers had learned to use bronze tools and weapons. The divided tribes eventually merged into kingdoms. In the fourth century BC, the Iron Age had developed. Each tribe learned to make pottery in the style characteristic of their culture.

Gojosean was the first kingdom in Korea. It was located in the north of the peninsula. Chinese records, in a text called the *Guanzi*, mention this kingdom. The first three kingdoms in Korea were Silla, Goguryeo, and Baekje. These three separate kingdoms eventually joined forces.

The Silla of 57 BC was founded by Bak Hyeokgeose. Goguryeo was founded by Juneong in 37 BC, and Baekje was founded by Onjo in 18 BC. These kingdoms were heavily influenced by the Chinese. The three kingdoms fought for power and supremacy. China tried twice to conquer the northern Korean kingdom.

The Kwbaek Council, which consisted of Korean nobles, dominated the government. They were powerful and had the ability to decide who would succeed to the throne. At that time, democratic voting of leaders did not exist. Only men were allowed to succeed to the throne.

The indigenous religion on the Korean peninsula followed the belief of Shamanism, which is the worship of nature and ancestors. Chandogyo, which combines "Eastern Learning," also known as the "Religion of the Heavenly Way," is also an indigenous religion of Korea. The following religions have numerous members: Buddhism, a philosophical form of religion, was brought into Korea from China. Buddhism teaches salvation through rebirth and enlightenment. Confucianism was also brought in from China to help establish social and political order.

There are believers of other religious faiths that have numerous followers in Korea. Christian religions of Protestantism and Catholicism have a presence in Korea. Islam and Daoism worshippers are also found on the peninsula. It is accepted to be an atheist and have no religious affiliation.

Silk became an export of Korea. In the seventh century, China sought Korean gold-workers. During 1101 A.D., silver vases were made and used as currency at the national level in Korea. The leader, Jogejeon, led a rebellion in 1126 but was not successful.

In 1258, peace was made with the Mongolian Empire. During 1592–1598, there were invasions of the Korean Empire by Japanese forces. These were times of rebellion followed by intervals of peace before new conflicts developed. Many of the Korean structures were destroyed by the Japanese but were later rebuilt. Some of the palaces offer beautiful gardens.

There are many beautiful temples in Korea. The village of Bukchon is a village of traditional houses called hanoks. The hanoks existed during the Joseon Dynasty. During the 1800s, major changes in rice transplantation techniques were made. Improved irrigation systems were developed. Japanese warlords started uprisings, and once again Korea was threatened by Japan. The Japanese ruled Korea from 1910 to 1945.

On February 8, 1945, at the Yalta Conference, U.S. President Franklin Delano Roosevelt proposed to Russia's Joseph Stalin that Korea be placed in a three-way trusteeship. This was to be an alliance between the U.S., China, and the Soviet Union. This trusteeship was to exist for 20–30 years. The proposal was eventually dismissed.

In May of 1945, "the Eagle" was a joint operation led by Korea to appeal for recognition as an independent country to the United States. Harry S. Truman rebuffed the attempts for communication made by Korea's leader, Kim. The mission was halted after the bombing of Japan. In 1948, Korea split into two countries, North and South Korea.

South Korea has over fifty million people. South Korea's largest city is Seoul. There are more than ten million people living in the region of Seoul. The largest city in North Korea is Pyongyang, which is the capital. Although Korean is the main language, many people also speak Chinese, Japanese, and English.

South Korea has many radio and television networks. Both Korean nations have high-speed rail trains. There are many poor areas in both North and South Korea. The farmers struggle to compete with inexpensive foods from other countries. The government of the Republic of Korea was installed on August 15, 1948.

The first election was held under U.N. supervision. On June 25, 1950, seventy-five thousand North Korean People's Army troops passed the 38th parallel and invaded South Korea. About halfway through the war, Chinese troops joined the North Korean Army to fight against South Korea.

The conflict was supported by two global superpowers – the Soviet Union, which supported North Korea, and the United States, which supported South Korea. This conflict, never recognized as a war, resulted in nearly five million deaths. There are 7,000 U.S. soldiers still missing in action. Propaganda and media portrayals had an impact on the conflict.

There were two motion pictures made about the Korean War – *Pork Chop Hill*, made in 1950, and *The Manchurian Candidate*, made in 1962. Movie mogul Clint Eastwood, drafted into military service, made the comment, "I was drafted into the Korean War. None of us wanted to go." Eastwood spent time during the war serving as a lifeguard during training in California.

A little-known hero of the South during the Korean War was a mare known as "Reckless." She brought ammunition to soldiers and carried wounded men off the battlefield. There is a statue of this hero in the National Museum of the Marine Corps. There were many famous people involved during this conflict, which did not merit being called a war according to political dictates.

Harry S. Truman was president of the United States. The U.S. and United Nations forces were led by General Douglas MacArthur and General Matthew Ridgeway. MacArthur was relieved of his command later by Truman. Dean Acheson was secretary of state under Truman. Acheson chose the 38th parallel as the dividing line between North and South. The 38th parallel is now known as the Korean Demilitarized Zone. South Korea, called the Republic of Korea, occupies the lower half, and North Korea, called the Democratic People's Republic, occupies the upper half of the peninsula.

The North Korean forces were led by Choi Yong-Kun. General Mark W. Clark was commander of U.N. forces in Korea from 1952–1953. Syngman Rhee was the first democratically elected president of South Korea. He was a committed nationalist obsessed with the idea of ruling a unified, independent Korea. James Van Fleet served as General Ridgeway's field commander.

Kim Il Sung was the communist leader of North Korea. He served until his death in 1994. Issues that exist currently in South Korea concern the launching of ballistic missiles by North Korea. Kim Jong-un, leader of North Korea, has stated that he is only retaliating against the threats and alliance of military involvement between Japan, South Korea, and the United States. A current issue of lesser consequences for Korea, found in recent newscasts, concerns moves to ban dog meat on menus by 2027.

Chapter Thirteen:
The Empire of The Israelite Nation

"I will make unto you a great nation and I will bless you . . . and all peoples on earth will be blessed through you."

(Genesis 12:2-3)

The Israelites were descendants of Semitic tribes in ancient times. Israel was the name given to Jacob – Abraham's grandson – after he wrestled with an angel, or perhaps God himself. The region the Israelites called their homeland was given the name Canaan. As mentioned earlier, Canaan was the son of Shem and grandson of Noah.

Also, as mentioned earlier, Shem's name was later changed to Sem. Sem was the son of Noah. The term "Israelite" was originally found as an inscription carved on a stele (stone) found in Thebes, which in modern times is Luxor. This stele was erected by the Egyptian Pharaoh Merneptah, who reigned from 1213 to 1203 BC.

The Israelite history begins in the Late Bronze Age and continues to the Early Iron Age. The culture of the Israelites developed as an extension of the Canaanites. The Bible of the Hebrews (name given to describe the patriarch Abraham and his descendants) gives reference to the reigns of

King Saul, David, and Solomon. David and his son Solomon ruled over an area that was divided into two kingdoms – Israel and Judah. These kingdoms had emerged in the region of the Southern Levant. The Levant is the historical region of modern-day Syria.

The earliest evidence of the ancient Israelite religion dates back to the year 2000 BC. Organization for administrative and taxation purposes of the Israelite holdings was under a monarchy. The culture was dictated by tribal associations. Israel was inhabited by the tribe of Benjamin. The Israelite family defined the way that each individual fit into the greater society.

Land was passed down from one generation to the next. The first-born son was favored. Women were not considered heirs. A daughter was important if she could marry favorably. She was also capable of providing sons to help with the responsibilities.

Ancient Israel was patriarchal. The role of women was limited and subjective. If a male landowner had no son, he could adopt one to be his heir. Israelite women married in their teens and then went to live with their husband's families. These customs were prevalent in the culture.

Perhaps because history was written by men, little information is available on the lives of ordinary Israelite women. It was found, written on scrolls made of papyrus, that women had the right to own land and to bring cases to court. They could own livestock and participate in commercial transactions. Women were also allowed to attend synagogue services.

The Kingdom of Israel was conquered and destroyed by the Assyrians around 720 BC. Although the Kingdom of Judah survived, it became subject to the Assyrian Empire and then later to the Babylonian Empire. It was probably from being citizens of Judah that the people were referred to as Jews. The biblical account describes revolt against Babylon in 586 BC, which led to the destruction of Judah. This was under the rule of Nebuchadnezzar II, King of Babylon. The Jewish temple was destroyed, and the Jews were exiled to Babylon.

There was a later dispersion of Israelites out of their ancient homelands. This was called the "Diaspora." The Israelites were exiled and forced to settle in other parts of the world. They migrated from Israel, Anatolia, Babylon, and Alexandria. They settled in Rome and in the territories of Roman Europe.

The Israelite or Jewish communities thrived economically in Rome. The Roman general Pompey conquered Jerusalem in 63 BC. Pompey deposed the ruling Hasmonean dynasty of Judea. The Roman Senate declared Herod the Great, King of the Jews.

Jesus honored his Jewish heritage. He was born to a Jewish mother, and his adopted father, Joseph, was a Jew. All of Jesus' friends, associates, colleagues, and disciples were Jews. Jesus observed the Jewish feast days, laws, and traditions. His first miracle was performed at a Jewish wedding. The history of the Israelite nation includes centuries of leadership, conflict, faith, and the resilience of God's chosen people.

Chapter Fourteen:
The Akkadian Empire

"Like Nimrod, a mighty hunter before the Lord. The first centers of his kingdom were Babylon, Erech, Akkad and Caineh . . ."

(Genesis 10:9-10)

One of the first kings of the Akkadian Empire was Nimrod. This empire reached its zenith during the 24th–22nd centuries BC. King Nimrod has been identified as the same person as Sargon, King of Akkad. The location of Akkad is placed in the area where the Tigris and Euphrates Rivers converge.

The Akkadian Empire brought a number of "firsts," which included setting a standard for the form of government in the ancient empires. Although little is known about the first of the Mesopotamian settlements, there existed a city-state known as Agade. This territory was also referred to as Akkad. King Sargon, a mighty warrior, united the separate kingdoms under a central authority.

Sargon never knew his father, according to his biography found on a clay tablet. Supposedly, he was placed in a basket and set afloat on the Euphrates River and found by a man named Akki. He was raised by this man. As he grew, Sargon became wise and accomplished in the military arts.

Sargon lived to conquer all of Mesopotamia. He was given the title "Sargon the Great." The government of the Sargon dynasty commanded obedience by ruling justly and serving as representatives of the gods. The Dynasty of Sargon ruled through his grandson until deposed by the Gutian Dynasty. Sargon was the father of the great poet-priestess, Enheduanna.

Chapter Fifteen:
The Babylonian Empire

"I will send foreigners to Babylon to winnow her and devastate her land."

(Jeremiah 51:2)

There is no mention in historical documents of Babylon before the twenty-third century BC. Babylon existed as an independent kingdom from the nineteenth century until its fall in the sixth century BC. It became the center of the small kingdom of King Sumuabum in 1894 BC. Babylon ruled the ancient kingdoms of Sumer and Akkad.

Babylon was located in south-central Mesopotamia. From the second millennium BC, Babylon was the capital of southern Mesopotamia. It was also the capital of the Chaldean region during the greatest time of the Babylonian reign—the seventh and sixth centuries BC. There are extensive ruins, which are probably Babylonian, on the Euphrates River, fifty-five miles south of Baghdad, near the town of Al-Hillak, Iraq.

After a raid by the Hittites in 1595 BC, control passed to the Kassites in 1570 BC. The Kassites remained in control for four centuries. The chief god was Marduk. In 1158 BC, Babylon was conquered by the Elamites under the rule of Nebuchadnezzar, who made it the capital of the kingdom.

Just before the year 1000 BC, pressure from northern Syria brought dissension among the administrators, between the Aramean and Chaldean tribesmen, for political control of the city. Nebuchadnezzar's Babylon was the largest kingdom in the world. The grandest feature was the great temple of Marduk with its ziggurat tower. King Sennacherib's "Hanging Gardens of Babylon" were also of notable fame.

King Belshazzar of Babylon gave a great banquet for a thousand of his nobles. He ordered gold and silver goblets that he had taken from the temple to be brought in so he and the nobles could drink from them. Daniel 5:4 states:

"As they drank the wine, they praised the gods of gold and silver, of bronze, iron, wood and stone. Suddenly the fingers of a human hand appeared and wrote on the plaster of the wall, near the lampstand in the royal palace. The king watched the hand as it wrote."

The king trembled and turned pale. So, Daniel, who had the ability to interpret dreams, explain riddles, and solve difficult problems, was brought in to interpret the writing on the wall. Daniel had been brought from the conquered Judah to Babylon. He had been chosen, along with three of his friends, to be put in the king's service in hopes of becoming assimilated into the Babylonian culture.

Daniel refused gifts offered by the king but agreed to interpret the writing on the wall:

"You praised the gods of silver and gold, of bronze, iron, wood and stone, which cannot see, hear or understand. But you did not honor the God who holds in His hand your life and all your ways. Therefore, he sent the hand that wrote the inscription . . . This is what these words mean: God has numbered the days of your reign and brought it to an end. You have been weighed on the scales and found wanting. Your kingdom has been divided and given to the Medes and the Persians."

(Daniel 5:26-28)

When night fell, Belshazzar was slain and his kingdom taken over by Darius, a Mede. The hierarchy of the king's court feared the favoritism shown to Daniel and attempted to find fault in him. They finally thought of a way to trap Daniel. They encouraged the king to forbid that anyone pray to anyone but the king.

Of course, Daniel would not pray to anyone but God. He was thrown, overnight, into the lion's den. When King Darius went to the lion's den the next morning and called out to Daniel, he was answered. Daniel had not been harmed by the lions.

Chapter Sixteen:
The Egyptian Empire

". . . so the King of Assyria will lead away stripped and barefoot the Egyptian captives and Cushite exiles, young and old, with buttocks bared – to Egypt's shame."

(Isaiah 20:4)

For over three thousand years, Egypt was the most important civilization in the Mediterranean world. A complete field of study—"Egyptology"—is devoted to the details of the pyramids, artifacts, government, and history of the Egyptian dynasties. This study is filled with artifacts from archaeological sites that depict a culture with few equals in art, pictographs, hieroglyphics, and architecture. The Bible offers the most interesting account of Joseph, the son of Jacob, who was the grandson of Abraham.

Joseph was the firstborn of Rachel and the favorite son of Jacob. Jacob had given Joseph a magnificent coat of many colors. This caused Joseph's brothers to be very jealous of him. They wanted to do harm to Joseph because of the attention Jacob gave him, so they began to plot ways to make him disappear.

Fifteen miles north of Shechem was the city of Dothan, which was on the main trade route leading through the Jezreel Valley to Egypt. Joseph and his brothers were tending their father's flocks in this area. The brothers stripped Joseph and put him in a dry cistern to hold him until they figured out what to do with him. Judah suggested to the brothers that they sell him to the Ishmaelites.

In the story from Genesis, there is the inference that just as Ishmael was sent as a fugitive into Sinai, so too would Joseph be sent as an enslaved person into the great kingdom of Egypt. The brothers thought up a story to tell their father, Jacob, about what had happened to Joseph. They slaughtered a goat and poured the blood on Joseph's precious coat. The brothers then told their father that a wild animal had devoured Joseph.

The truth was that the brothers sold Joseph to a caravan of traders traveling to Egypt. Upon arrival in Egypt, Joseph was put to work in the house of Potiphar, who was employed by Pharaoh's guard. Joseph became known as one who could interpret dreams. Pharaoh had a dream that could not be interpreted by any of his magicians.

As Joseph was known for interpreting dreams, he was sent for by advisers to Pharaoh. He warned Pharaoh of a great famine that would sweep over the land, causing hardship and death. He explained to Pharaoh that there would be seven years of plenty and then seven years of drought. Joseph suggested that Pharaoh find someone who was wise and capable to make plans to prepare for the lean years. Joseph, the Hebrew slave and son of Jacob, became the head vizier of the great kingdom of Egypt.

Among the people from all over the land who streamed into Egypt to buy food were Joseph's brothers. They did not recognize Joseph, so he put them to a test. Benjamin was arrested and came before the grand vizier, Joseph. Joseph was overwhelmed and told his brothers who he was and pardoned them for what they had done to him.

They sent for Jacob, all his wives, servants, and livestock to come to Egypt. Pharaoh settled the tribal family of Joseph in the land of Goshen. This land was in the northeastern part of the fertile Nile Delta. The Israelites prospered in the land of Goshen. The soil was suitable for tilling. There were pastures for grazing the large herds owned by Joseph's people. Their diet consisted of fish, lamb, lentils, cabbage, barley, and wheat to make bread.

The Israelite shepherds added the agrarian lifestyle as a means to survive in the new kingdom. During the period of 1780 to 1550 BC, the nomadic wanderers from Syria and Canaan settled into the Nile Delta. They were known as the Hyksos (Hykau-khoswet), meaning "desert princes." It is at this point that the stories told in the book of Genesis come to a close.

There were many rulers of the kingdoms in the larger empire of Egypt. There were six powerful female rulers in Egypt's history. Many of the wives of rulers played important political and religious roles. Nefertiti and King Akhenaten ruled Egypt together from 1353 to 1336 BC. They were best known for getting the citizenry into monotheistic beliefs. They encouraged the worship of only one god—the sun god called Aten.

In the temples erected in Karnack, Nefertiti is presented in artwork scenes more times than her husband. She was known as the "goddess of fertility."

It was during this time that the Egyptians developed a reverence for the dead and the belief in a hereafter. The only other female to rival Nefertiti was Cleopatra.

The tomb of Mernaith, a female Pharaoh, goes down in history as an equal to that of the kings of the first dynasty. She could possibly have been a ruler in her own right. Hatshepsut is the second historically confirmed female ruler of Egypt. She married her half-brother, Thutmose II, at the age of twelve. Hatshepsut became queen. When Thutmose II died, she became regent to her infant stepson.

The last known ruler of the 19th dynasty was Queen Twosret. She gained control of the throne and declared herself pharaoh upon the death of her stepson, Siptah. Either her reign ended in civil war or war erupted upon her death. Her reign was between 1191 and 1189 BC.

Probably the most famous female pharaoh was Cleopatra VII Philopator, whose reign was from 51–12 BC. She was from a family of Macedonian Greek origin. Cleopatra led at the side of her father and then later ruled with her brothers. She could speak six languages fluently.

When she became eighteen, Cleopatra married Ptolemy XIII but would not share power with him. She would not let him sign documents and did not let his picture appear on any currency. She only allowed her image to appear on Egyptian currency.

Chapter Seventeen:
The Assyrian Empire

"The Assyrians came down like the wolf on the fold,

And their cohorts were gleaming in purple and gold;

And the sheen of their spears was like stars on the sea,

When the blue wave rolls nightly on deep Galilee."

~Lord Byron

The above quote is a verse from Lord Byron's poem about Sennacherib, King of Assyria, whose siege of Jerusalem was overthrown by the Lord. This incident occurred following the prayers of Hezekiah, King of Judah, who consulted with Isaiah, the prophet. An angel was sent by the Lord to kill Sennacherib's soldiers, who numbered one hundred and eighty-five thousand, including the leaders and officers. This occurred in 701 BC.

Sennacherib withdrew in disgrace and returned to his own land. He went into the temple of his god. It was there that he was killed by his sons. This was a testimony to the Creator of heaven and earth. Jerusalem was the daughter of Zion (the highest point of rule) and therefore protected by the Father – God.

Isaiah was a prophet of the Old Testament, whose name means "Yahweh is salvation." His prophecies were profound and are still meaningful in present times. Isaiah predicted the coming of a Messiah hundreds of years before Jesus was born. The apostle Matthew quoted Isaiah when he described John the Baptist's ministry.

Jesus also quoted Isaiah's prophecy when speaking in parables. Jesus read from the Book of Isaiah in the synagogue at Nazareth. He claimed that Isaiah's prophecy was fulfilled in him. Paul, found in Acts 28:26-27, also uses the same quote as Jesus from the Book of Isaiah.

Isaiah is called "the Prince of Prophets." The Gospels (Matthew, Mark, Luke, and John) quote more from the prophecies of Isaiah than any other prophet. Isaiah was the son of Amoz. The accounts revealed in the Book of Isaiah inform us of what was going on at that time in biblical history.

The prophet Isaiah was also a preacher. His call to prophecy in 742 BC was the beginning of the westward expansion of the Assyrian Empire. This expansion was a threat to Israel. Isaiah proclaimed that, "prophecies were a warning from God to a godless people."

Isaiah prophesied under the rule of four kings of Judah: Uzziah, Jotham, Ahaz, and Hezekiah. In his prophecies, Isaiah presents oracles against many nations: Babylon, Assyria, Philistine, Moab, Syria, Israel, Ethiopia, Egypt, Cush, and Arabia. An oracle, in historical antiquity, was a person or agency that offered wise and insightful counsel and predictions for the future. Personally, I believe with all of my heart that the Holy Word of God is meant to be for all times; it is meant to be observed in today's world.

God's Holy Writ, the Bible, contains the commandments that we are to live by. It describes the way we are to take care of the land, the animals He placed in the Garden of Eden, and how to take care of ourselves. God tells how we are to love ourselves and our neighbor. There is no aspect in the world, or of the world, that is not addressed in the Holy Bible.

It is my belief that the prophecies of Isaiah are a warning to the world at this very moment in time. I believe, from the depths of my heart, that America, the land that I love, is in jeopardy of the same fate as those previous empires that fell because the people turned away from God.

As we return to the story of Isaiah and the King of Jerusalem, we learn that Hezekiah remained faithful to the Lord. When illness came upon him and death seemed near, Hezekiah pleaded with the Lord for more time on earth. The Lord heard Hezekiah's prayer and gave him fifteen more years. Like King David, Hezekiah was faithful to the Lord.

From the ninth to the seventh century BC, the capital of this early biblical region was Nineveh. The city of Nineveh was so large that it took three days to travel around the circumference of it. The Assyrians were fierce and cruel and showed little mercy to those they conquered.

The Assyrian history begins under King Tilgath-Pilesar. Mesopotamia existed from the 21st century until the 14th century BC. Following the

Mesopotamian Empire began the formation of the Assyrian Empire. Ashur-Uballit I, a former general, reigned as king during the Assyrian feudal age. The form of government by which Assyria was ruled was that of a monarchy.

Assyria existed from the Bronze Age to the Iron Age. Like most empires, it grew by conquest through warfare. The development of iron weapons, which were superior to those of bronze, and better strategies and tactics advanced the Assyrian armies to the status of the most powerful military force of its time. This mighty military developed many maneuvers and weapons by which they conquered every opposing enemy with which they engaged.

The Assyrian Empire was the first to utilize groups of men to engineer the construction of warfare weapons and machines to combat their enemies. These engineers constructed ladders to assist soldiers in climbing over the walls surrounding great fortresses. It was the Assyrians who invented the wheel. The engineers also developed a tank-type vehicle to protect the soldiers as they advanced toward the fortress of their enemy.

The religion of Assyria was pagan and hosted a pantheon of gods. There were approximately 2,400 gods and goddesses. Sometimes a city had a specific god for whom they erected a temple that contained altars of worship and sacrifice. The king served as the leader and priest of the people.

Chapter Eighteen:
The Greek or Hellenistic Empire

". . . to those whom God has called, both Jews and Greeks, Christ is the power of God and the wisdom of God."

(I Corinthians I:24)

The original Greek holdings consisted of over 1,500 city-states. The city-states banded together against their common enemy—the Persians. In 507 BC, under the leadership of Cleisthenes, the city of Athens developed a system of popular rule called democracy. The assembly (Ecclesia) consisted of all male citizens.

The inhabitants of the Greek civilization shared many cultural traits. They shared a polytheistic religion—a religion of many gods—and a language with many dialects. These Greek pagan deities were called the Olympian gods. The religious beliefs of Ancient Greece included stories about supernatural beings of varied forms. Their pagan worship included rituals and cult practices. There was no word in the early Greek language for "religion."

Herodotus lived during the era of 484–425 BC. He was a Greek historian and geographer. He was known for having written a detailed account of the Greco-Persian Wars. Historians report that he was known to extensively research the details of the information about which he was writing. This endeavor earned him the title of "The Father of History."

Philosophies such as Stoicism and some forms of Platonism imply, by the use of the language found in writings, the assumption of one God. Stoicism is a philosophy that asserts that the practice of virtue is both necessary and sufficient to achieve happiness. Stoicism also advocates that what you say is not as important as what you do. Another proponent of Stoicism is that you must understand nature.

The Ancient Greek Civilization grew into an empire that spanned over a thousand years. It began with the rise of city-states such as Athens and Sparta. It was common for these city-states to be ruled through tyranny and oligarchy, which means "by many kings."

The term "polis" was given to the city-states of the Ancient Greek Kingdom. We have adopted the use of this term in the expression "metropolis," which means a large populated area. The first date recorded in Greek history is 776 BC, which is the year of the first Olympic Games. The names of the victors who took part in the Olympics were recorded. The competitive activities of the Olympics were referred to as "peer polity interaction."

Artifacts found in the late twentieth century on an island site in the Bay of Naples reveal Ancient Greek inscriptions. There are also artifacts which indicate an exchange of goods between Ancient Greece and the inhabitants of Italy and Sicily. This exchange occurred before 750 BC. Thucydides, a historian of the fifth century BC, wrote a synopsis of Greek history from the Trojan War to his day. He stated that "Greece is gradually settling down," which implied that fewer wars were being initiated.

The Greek Civilization contributed great literature such as Homer's *Iliad* and the *Odyssey*. The Athenian Acropolis is a building of renown that has remains that survived until the present time. This building memorialized the deities of the Greek civilization. Other remains of original architecture are the Parthenon, Temple of Herodes Atticus, and the separate Temples of Hera, Artemis, and Apollo.

The period of 900 BC is called by historians of Ancient Empires "The Dark Ages of Greece." It was a time of unrest, indecisiveness, and regrouping for the city-states of this rising empire. It was after this time that Greece acquired, through conquest and political negotiations, the colonies of Italy, Sicily, and what is now Western Turkey. Archaeological artifacts have been uncovered in these areas.

One of the greatest leaders of Greece was Alexander the Great. He was able to expand the Greek Empire to the reaches of India and Asia. Alexander was the son of Philip II of Macedonia. He was a general who did not lose a single battle.

Alexander the Great changed the course of history. He studied under Aristotle. Alexander supposedly placed a copy of Homer's *Iliad*, annotated by Aristotle, along with his dagger, under his pillow at night. He became king of Macedonia at the age of twenty. Alexander served for almost thirteen years.

During his travels to China, Alexander saw peacocks for the first time. He brought some of the beautiful birds back to Greece with him. The colorful, iridescent feathers of the peacock became the symbol of his power. It is believed that several prophets had visions of Alexander the Great many centuries before he was born. Alexander believed in the polytheistic gods worshipped in Greece at that time.

His campaigns greatly increased trade between the East and the West. Some of the cities he established became major cultural centers that are still in existence in the twenty-first century. He became ill and died after a lengthy, festive banquet offering rich foods and strong drinks. Some historians say his death was brought about by his own army, who insisted on traveling back home. Alexander the Great was considered a god to many followers. When Alexander died in 323 BC, the Greek Empire was divided into four territories and given to his generals.

In the second century BC, the Roman Empire annexed Greece. The Hellenistic culture influenced its colonies and made its mark in the areas of the arts, literature, theater, architecture, music, mathematics, philosophy, and science. This Mediterranean civilization existed from the Greek Dark Ages to the Middle Ages. Economic and political instability caused large-scale revolts in some of the eastern Mediterranean areas.

There were attempts made to overthrow some of the more powerful kingdoms by surrounding tribes. A group of attacking enemies was known as the "Sea People." They were from the Black Sea, the Aegean, and the Anatolian regions. Information on the "Sea People" was recorded in Egyptian military successes.

Western civilization has been greatly influenced by Greek political forms of government. Greek pottery and sculpture have inspired artists for thousands of years. Greek poetry, epics, and lyrics are still read around the world. The Judeo-Christian Bible tells of happenings in the Greek culture.

Upon hearing Paul's words in Philippi, Lydia of Thyatira becomes the first convert to Christianity in Europe. Paul writes two Epistles to the Thessalonians in Corinth, Greece. He converted Proconsul Sergius on his second mission trip. This served as an example for others to follow because of Sergius' position as a leader.

Much of our language has its origin in Greek words—*agoraphobia*, which means "fear of crowded places," refers to the immense Greek Agora market. Paul, sometimes referred to as the thirteenth apostle, was sent on three mission trips to spread the word of Jesus to the entire world. On his second mission trip, Paul went to Greece. This occurred in 49 AD. Paul went to Athens, the home of Plato's Academy, Aristotle's Lyceum, and the birthplace of democracy. When I traveled to Greece, I was able to visit the Agora market and found it very interesting and educational.

Paul went to preach in the Agora, which is an open-air market still in existence in Athens today. He was not met by eager listeners. The people were predominantly pagans and did not want to hear about the man called Jesus, who was resurrected from the dead. A group of Athenians took Paul to the Areopagus, the high court of Athens.

Paul was able to preach there. He had discussions with Epicurean and Stoic philosophers. Because of his parents and his place of birth, Paul was a Roman citizen and well educated. Although the Greeks were pagans, the people Paul was talking to were well educated in matters of the world.

Paul explained the meaning of "believing in one God" and asked his listeners to get to know this God, Sovereign of the creation, who was in charge of all the areas that were represented by the various deities of the pagan world. Hierotheos, the Thesmothete, a member of the Areopagus, was converted to Christianity by Paul and became the Bishop of Athens. Hierotheos converted many to Christianity. He later died a martyr's death.

Paul arrived in Macedonia with Silas and Luke in the winter of 49 AD. Although Paul, Luke, and Silas were arrested and thrown in prison, they received God's help to escape.

"About midnight Paul and Silas were praying, And singing hymns to God, and the other prisoners were listening to them. Suddenly there was such a violent earthquake that the foundations of the prison were shaken, At once all the prison doors flew open, and everybody's chains came loose. The jailer woke up, and when he saw the prison doors open, he drew his sword and was about to kill himself because he thought the prisoners had escaped. But Paul shouted, 'Don't harm yourself. We are all here!' The jailer called for lights, rushed in and fell trembling before Paul and Silas. He then brought them out and asked, 'Sirs, what must I do to be saved?'"

(Acts 16:25-30)

The apostle Paul made a mission trip to Greece and Cyprus in the Apostolic Era during the early fifties, AD.

Chapter Nineteen:
The Persian Empire

*"In the third year of Cyrus king of Persia, a revelation was given to
Daniel. Its message was true and it concerned a great war."*

(Daniel 10:1-2)

The Persian Empire, founded by Cyrus the Great, reached from the eastern
Mediterranean Sea to the western border of India. This empire was founded
in 550 BC. The Persian Empire included a diversity of cultures and ethnic
groups. It became one of the largest empires in history.

The words of King Cyrus, found in II Chronicles 36:23, state:

*"The Lord, God of heaven, has given me all the kingdoms of the earth
and has appointed me to build a temple for him at Jerusalem in Judah.
Anyone of his people among you – may the Lord his God be with him, and
let him go up."*

It was through the efforts of Cyrus, king of Persia, that the Hebrews could
return to Judah, after a captivity of seventy years, to rebuild the temple. A
priest and Jewish leader by the name of Ezra helped the people become a
community through their religious beliefs, as found in the Torah. The
people had fallen away from the laws of Moses. Ezra taught the Hebrews
that, although they were scattered all over the earth, they could survive as

a community of like believers. This philosophy has continued, and the Jewish community remains united in their beliefs and form of worshipping God.

Ezra has been referred to by some historians as a second Moses.

This religious leader re-established worship through spiritual revival and initiating reforms. These reforms projected the need for recognition as a religious community and for believers to show the world they were God's chosen people. Ezra encouraged the chosen people of God to make worship a top priority in their lives.

This concept has been proven centuries later through many wars and is still representative of the Jewish communities of modern times. Ezra wanted the people to realize how essential the Word of God was to the nation and to them personally. The Word of God is the same in these modern times. The Holy Spirit of God must dwell in the believer's heart if we are to become ambassadors of God.

The Persian Empire was made up of a series of dynasties, with the center existing in Persia, which reached from Europe's Balkan Peninsula in the west to India's valley in the east. Later it branched out into regions that became Pakistan, Afghanistan, Tajikistan, and Azerbaijan. The Persian Empire was established over 2,700 years ago.

This great empire existed from 559 to 331 BC. The Persians were the first to implement a policy for human rights. The Persian Empire was one of the most scientific civilizations among the ancient empires. History reveals the vast contributions of this empire. Perhaps the greatest contribution of the Persian Empire was the Hebrew nation's recognition of God as being worthy of worship.

It was during the age of the Persian Empire that many inventions were developed. We acknowledge the Persians for creating the first map. Maps were immensely helpful during the campaigns of war. Explorers have depended on maps to describe the location of lands discovered during their explorations.

The world's first map was created by a Persian cartographer who carved a map on a clay tablet in 2,300 BC. This map was of a small area of the Akkadian Empire. The map indicated trade routes that were used during hunting, military altercations, and exploration. Great details were given in the drawing of this map.

The map presents the world as circular and indicates rivers, canals, swamps, and mountains. It has seven small circles representing the seven cities found in Babylon. It is one of the most interesting items from that era. This map is found in the British Museum.

The Cuneiform alphabet, originating in 3,400 BC, is the first known form of written communication. It was comprised of 1,000 characters and was used in the accounting of business matters and administrative purposes. It was an important tool in educational situations. It was also used in discussing astrological occurrences.

These characters were used extensively in technical situations for writing medical papers and mathematical derivations. A stylus with a fine point was used to carve characters on a clay tablet to make and maintain records. The ancient Iraqi language, as well as the Akkadian and Sumerian languages, were similarly carved on clay slabs.

The Persians also developed a primitive form of plow. This was the hoe, which was the first tool to be used to till the soil in preparation for planting seeds. Agriculture was a necessary practice for survival in the early cultures. Agriculture was not only essential in feeding the people but also provided a means of employment.

Since the earth dried up quickly, the invention of the stone plow was a helpful invention. Crops such as wheat, barley, and lentils were grown as essential foods. Flax was grown to be used to make clothing. These were the standard crops of this time.

Canals and irrigation ditches were dug to water these crops. The control of the flow of water was very beneficial for maintaining the growth of crops. There were high mountains in the Persian Empire that were capped with snow and ice. The Persians made use of this natural condition and constructed structures to preserve food.

These structures were the first ice boxes. They were called "yakhchals." "Yakh" means ice, and "chal" means pit. The Persians mastered the construction of the yakhchal and brilliantly developed an evaporation cooler to store foods over the summer months. They used batteries made of sulfuric acid as a source of energy.

The ice box looked like a giant terra-cotta flowerpot turned upside down, sitting on a basement structure dug into the earth. The above-ground structure was used to store the food needed to survive during the hot months of summer. The subterranean space was used to store the ice and hold the evaporation equipment. The yakhchals were large, round structures. Since large stones were scarce, bricks were made out of clay. The walls were approximately two meters thick. These first ice boxes improved the quality of living in this ancient empire.

Chapter Twenty:
The Early Roman Empire

"They will fall by the edge of the sword and be led captive among all nations, and Jerusalem will be trampled underfoot by the Gentiles, until the times of the Gentiles are fulfilled."

(Luke 21:24)

Julius Caesar was a politician and Roman general who led the Roman military in the Gallic Wars. Caesar defeated Pompey in a civil war and became dictator of the Roman Republic from 49 BC until 44 BC. He played a leading role in the fall of the Roman Republic and the rise of the Roman Empire. He was stabbed to death in 44 BC.

In the middle of the first century BC, unrest built up, and civil war erupted. This war was fought between leaders Julius Caesar and Pompey Strabo. Battles continued between Octavian and Marc Antony. Octavian was the victor and was made Imperator. He was awarded the name Augustus and ruled as emperor.

The Early Roman Empire had gained large holdings around the Mediterranean Sea. Holdings also existed in Europe, North Africa, and Western Asia. The city-states were ruled by kings, while the empire was ruled by an emperor. In the case of the Roman Empire, the governing leader was referred to as "Caesar."

Business, political, and governmental affairs were centered in Rome. The Roman Empire expanded until it covered 1.7 million acres. It was the goal of the Roman Empire to conquer the world. Caesar Augustus was the first Roman emperor. There was a stable and relatively peaceful period referred to as "Pax Romana." This term meant "Roman Peace."

There were a thousand years of order under the rule of the Romans. This time in the history of the Early Roman Empire was one of tranquility. The empire protected and governed the individual provinces. Each province was allowed to make and administer its own laws. Every province was under taxation by the central government in Rome.

The Romans worshipped various gods. There was a god for every important aspect of their existence. Many people had shrines in their homes to pay tribute to the gods. Their belief was that if you were good to the gods, they would reward you.

Jesus, the Son of God, began his ministry during the rule of Pontius Pilate, governor of Judea who held office during 26–36 AD. Judea was under Roman rule. Jesus was the son of Mary, a Jewish girl, who was pregnant through the Holy Spirit.

"This is how the birth of Jesus Christ came about: His mother Mary was pledged to be married to Joseph but before they came together, she was

found to be with child through the Holy Spirit."

(Matthew 1:18)

Her son was adopted by her betrothed, Joseph. The crucifixion of Christ and resurrection from the grave, occurred at this time in history. The birth, crucifixion and resurrection of Jesus changed the history of the world.

"There was a violent earthquake, for an angel from the Lord came down from heaven and, going to the tomb, rolled back the stone and sat on it. His appearance was like lightening and his clothes were white as snow."
(Matthew 28:2-3)

The Emperor Constantine, in 313 AD, issued the Edict of Milan, which recognized Christianity. Ten years after this edict, Christianity became the official religion of the Roman Empire. The Roman Empire split into Eastern and Western divisions. Later, the Visigoths conquered the Roman Empire.

The Western Roman Empire slowly declined, and by 476 AD no longer existed. The nobles fled the capital and lived in their provincial estates. Many citizens owned slaves to perform great tasks. There was no single event, no designated war, or cataclysmic event that caused the fall of the Western Roman Empire.

There were 1,000 years of order under the rule of the Caesars. Several factors contributed to forming a chasm that developed into the gradual decline of the Roman Empire. The date of the fall of the Roman Empire is difficult to ascertain in history. The fall is usually associated with the Byzantine Emperor, Justinian.

Emperor Romulus was deposed in 476 AD and replaced. The following five factors contributed to the fall of the Roman Empire:

1. Internal strife and low confidence in the empire. Social issues existed. There were thirty thousand prostitutes in Rome.
2. Economic deterioration existed that made it difficult to finance the many facets of government. The state treasury was constantly drained.
3. The empire was split into two contingencies – the Eastern Roman Empire, called the Byzantine Empire, and the Western Roman Empire. There were rich and poor constituents, a famine ravished the people, and a decline in the population came about.
4. The military was weakened by overspending.
5. There were Barbarian invasions.

There was a decline in the morality of the people. Sexual perversion was rampant. Stories of sexual orgies at this time have been recorded in history. Assassinations of husbands, wives, and governmental leaders were common. It is this author's belief that history is repeating itself in many ways in today's world. Sexual relationships outside of marriage are not forbidden but appear to be socially acceptable. Assassination attempts have been made on the present president of the U.S. There is war in the Holy Land and in Ukraine.

As we continue the study of the Roman Empire, we learn that the third Roman Emperor, Caligula, was the son of Roman general Germanicus and Agrippina, Caesar Augustus' granddaughter. The name Caligula means "little boots." Caligula wore little army boots when he was with his father. He was responsible for carnage and waste during his four-year reign of the Roman Empire. It was questioned by many if Caligula was sane or possibly mad.

Chapter Twenty- One:
The Eastern Roman Empire – The Byzantine Empire

"Justice is the firm and continuous desire to render to everyone that which is his due."

~Justinian I, Byzantine Emperor

After the fall of the Western Roman Empire, the eastern division of the empire survived the conditions that toppled its western counterpart. The Eastern Roman Empire continued to exist from the 5th century AD until the 14th century. It was the most powerful economic and cultural force in the Mediterranean. It also had the strongest military at that time.

The citizenry of the Eastern Roman Empire referred to themselves as Romans. The Greek language and cultural traditions became the predominant forces. The Eastern Roman Empire became the center for intellectual, cultural, and financial aspects of the Roman Empire.

Churches were constructed in Byzantine architectural designs that included many domes placed on top of round, square, or rectangular structural bases. On the undersides of the domes, inside the churches, Byzantine art in the form of frescoes and mosaics featured Christ, the Pantocrator (ruler of the universe), at the top of the church dome. There were angels painted at the base of the dome. The Virgin Mary was often presented in another dome scene. The lowest realm of the scene was that of the church congregation. The whole church suggested a microcosm of the universe.

The capital of the Eastern Roman Empire was moved from Rome to Byzantium in 330 AD. The name of the city was changed to Constantinople. The Byzantine Empire was centered in Constantinople. In 380 AD, Emperor Theodosius I declared Christianity the official religion. Constantinople became the center for theological development. The religious leaders of the Byzantine Empire held many debates and councils.

These discussions resulted in the formation of the Nicene Creed. This creed is also called "The Creed of Constantinople." The Nicene Creed is a formal statement of Christian beliefs adopted in 325 AD by the First Ecumenical Council. It is still recited in many church worship services.

In the fourth century, Attila the Hun ravaged the regions of the Roman Empire. He demanded a massive payment for peace. The followers of Attila broke up after his death in 453. The warlord Odoacer deposed Romulus Augustulus in 476. The Eastern Roman Empire was never ruled by barbarian vassals.

A dispute arose over the public use of religious images. This was based on the biblical scripture from Exodus 20:4,

"You shall not make for yourself a carved image, or any likeness of anything that is in heaven above, or that is in the earth below, or that is in the water under the earth."

In 726, Emperor Leo III took a stand against the worship of icons. In 730, he prohibited their use. Those people who continued using icons during the reign of his successor, Constantine VI, were persecuted. This act was revoked by Empress Irene in the Seventh Ecumenical Council of Nicea.

In the eighth century AD, Charlemagne was crowned Roman Emperor. The Roman Empire experienced several periods of decline and recovery. The plague and devastating wars depleted the resources of the empire. Egypt and Syria, the empire's richest provinces, were lost to the Muslim Rashidun Caliphate.

This resulted in a decrease of power in the flailing empire. Its territories were divided and progressively annexed by the Ottomans. Many refugees settled in Italy and other areas in Europe. The Eastern Roman Empire struggled as many wars were fought in the 14th and 15th centuries.

Religion shaped all aspects of Byzantine life. Christianity was encouraged by Constantine's support. Disputes split the churches of the Eastern and Western Empires into branches – Chalcedonian, Monophysite, and Nestorian. The Christian Chalcedonian branch dominated the territories of the Eastern Empire.

The Monophysite and Nestorian branches fell under Muslim rule. This resulted in the rise of Islam in the 7th century. Constantinople was the largest and most wealthy city in Europe until the 13th century. Constantinople was first called Byzantium, then Constantinople, and is now known as Istanbul.

The last Byzantine emperor, Constantine XI, after a two-month siege of Constantinople, cast off his imperial regalia and threw himself into hand-to-hand combat after the enemy entered the walled city. As many as twenty-seven million people lived in Byzantium at its peak. By the time the Turks captured Constantinople, there were only two million people living in the city. The Eastern Roman Empire was given the name "Byzantine" after its fall.

Chapter Twenty-Two:
The Ottoman Empire

"Better the Sultan's turban than the Cardinal's hat."

~Loukas Notaras

The author of the above quote was Prime Minister of the Roman court that dealt with the Ottomans. He was also the admiral of the naval fleet. The Ottoman Empire was founded in 1299 AD by Sultan Osman I. He had a dream in which he envisioned a conquest appearing like a tree with its roots spreading through three continents.

The branches of the tree covered the sky and shaded four mountain ranges: the Caucasus, the Taurus, the Atlas, and the Balkan ranges. The four rivers in this area were the Tigris, Euphrates, Nile, and the Danube. The official language of the Ottoman Empire was Turkish. The capitals of this empire were Sogut from 1302–1326, Bursa from 1326–1365, then Edirne from 1365–1452, and Byzantium, later Constantinople, from 1453–1922.

At its peak, the lands possessed by the Ottoman Empire covered 5,200,000 kilometers. The zenith of the Ottoman Empire was from the sixteenth to the eighteenth century. It controlled Southeast Europe, Southwest Asia, and North Africa. The strategic conquest of Constantinople in 1453 became crucial, as it ended the Byzantine Empire and cemented the Ottoman

Empire as a superpower in Southeastern Europe and the Eastern Mediterranean.

A guild of Ottoman educators expressing the philosophy of Theodicy, whereby God permits the manifestation of evil, denounced the newly invented printing press. They called it "The Devil's invention." This caused a fifty-three-year delay in the use of this invention in the Ottoman Empire. This, along with a period of failed reforms and the lowering of taxes, caused instability in the empire.

In 1786, Russia began to expand its borders, and troops entered the Ottoman-controlled city of Balta and burned it to the ground. This provoked the Ottomans into the first Russo-Turkish War of 1768–1774. Stagnation, reforms, and threats by the Austrian Empire and the Russians occurred between 1700 and 1827. Egypt and Algeria became independent. In the eighteenth century, centralized authority within the Ottoman Empire gave way to provincial autonomy of local governors and leaders. Charles XII persuaded Ottoman Sultan Ahmed III to declare war on Russia.

This resulted in the War of 1700–1721. The Treaty of Kuchuck Kainnarji brought a period of peace. This ended Ottoman control of the Black Sea. The treaty also allowed Russian diplomatic intervention into internal affairs of the Ottoman Empire.

Chapter Twenty-Three:
The Islamic Empire

"None of us truly believe, until we wish for our brother what we wish for ourselves."

~The Prophet, Mohammad (P.B.U.H)

Mohammad ibn Abdullah was an Arab. He was a religious and political leader. Mohammad was the founder of the Islamic religion. According to the Islamic faith, Mohammad was a prophet. This prophet lived in the time period of 570 to 632 A.D. Mohammad is also spelled "Muhammad."

From 636 to 1299 A.D., Babylon and Israel were under the rule of Caliphs. The Caliphates were the regions under the rule of a Caliph. The Caliphs were political-religious successors to the Islamic prophet, Mohammad. The ruling Caliph is the ruler of the entire Muslim world.

The prophet, Mohammad, appeared during the Rashidun Caliphate. Rashidun, or Rashdan, is the name given to a male child of the Islamic faith. In 637 A.D., Islamic armies conquered Israel and Babylon. The Islamic Empire became fragmented. The different city-states were ruled by regional powers.

After Mohammad died, Islam began to spread throughout the Arabian Peninsula. This was made possible through travel along the trade routes in that part of the world. Abu Bakr, a close friend of Mohammad, became the first leader, or Caliph, after Mohammad. Bakr and the next three leaders were called the "Four Rightly Guided" because they followed the dictates of Mohammad.

Islam began to spread throughout the Fertile Crescent in the Middle East to North Africa and Central Asia. The Umayyad family took power after the death of the "Fourth Rightly Guided Caliph," Abu. The Umayyad family expanded the Islamic Empire farther across North Africa and into Spain. The decision was made by the Umayyad family to move the capital of the Empire from Mecca to Damascus.

Chapter Twenty-Four:
The Empire of France

"How can you govern a country that has 246 varieties of cheese?"

~Charles de Gaulle, President of France

The first written records of the history of France appeared during the Iron Age. The people struggled as the territories grew. It was difficult to maintain order in this fragmented region of the world. Leaders emerged from internal conflicts and civil disorder. Warring conquests resulted in a difference in leadership.

The leaders protected the people from invaders who looted their settlements. In 600 B.C., the Greeks built the colony of Marsalia, which is present-day Marseille, on the shores of the Mediterranean Sea. This area was known to the Romans as Gaul. France is one of the oldest countries in the world. The early provinces were ruled by kings, bishops, dukes, and monks.

The Gauls were descendants of the Celtic people. The Celts were an Indo-European people who migrated across the land from Portugal to Turkey and then branched out to other places. In the late 2nd century B.C., Roman legions under Julius Caesar conquered Gaul during the Gallic Wars of 58–51 B.C. Gaul and its inhabitants merged into the Roman Empire.

In the early Roman Empire, Gaul was attacked by Germanic Franks, who became the dominant ruling power over Gaul for several hundred years. The Franks were from the Rhine area. The name Frank means "brave." The Franks converted from barbarianism to Christianity. The last raid ended with the establishment of a new empire known as West Francia.

France converted from pagan worship of many deities to Christianity and the worship of one God. God promises to be with His chosen people.

"Blessed is the nation whose God is the Lord, the people whom he has chosen as his heritage."

(Psalm 33:12)

It is my belief that it is because of this choice to follow the Word of God that France has survived many difficult situations and challenges. France not only survived, it thrived in spite of many problems. Charlemagne was king of the Franks and king of the Lombards. He was the first emperor of the Holy Roman Empire. He ruled much of Western Europe in the eighth century. Because of his military position, he spent the first three decades of his reign in battle against the Saxons.

Charlemagne appointed Frankish nobility to rule the territories of France. He introduced the payment of taxes by coin as a prerequisite of land ownership. Charlemagne, with his courage, strength, and iron will, did much to determine the shape and character of medieval Europe. Charlemagne is referred to as the "Father of Modern Europe." He was crowned by Pope Leo III in 800. Charlemagne had a lasting influence on Europe throughout the Early Middle Ages.

Paris, in November of 885, was under siege when hundreds of longships of the Vikings brought thousands of men, demanding everything of value. King Charles the Fat arrived to defend Paris, but instead of fighting the Vikings, he allowed them to sail up the Seine to Burgundy. The Vikings attacked Paris multiple times in the future. The last raid ended with the Vikings dragging their boats and pillage overland to the Marne, an eastern tributary of the Seine, to leave the country.

During the era of 936–973, Otto I established the Saxons (Northern German people) in control of France. He was able to appoint popes as rulers. He was known as "Otto the Great." Otto was an East Frankish German leader during the 900s and was crowned Roman Emperor.

Hugh Capet was the first king of France. He ruled until 996. The rulers were given the title "Rex Francorum" – king of the Franks. Capet was a descendant of Charlemagne and claimed descent from Constantine the Great.

He inherited vast estates in Paris and Orleans. Hugh Capet became one of the most powerful vassals in the kingdom. Much of Hugh Capet's life was spent fighting Charles I of Lower Lorraine. Hugh Capet was the first of a direct line of fourteen Capetian kings of France.

Our Lord provided instructions for us to be unified in every way possible. Jesus Christ prayed that His followers would be as one. This is found in John 17:22-23:

"I have given them the glory that you gave me, that they may be one even as we are one, I in them and you in me, that they may become perfectly one, so that the world may know that you sent me and love them even as you love me."

But the churches did not work as one. The Great Schism of 1054 was between the Church of Constantinople and the Church of Rome. The split was over political, cultural, theological, and liturgical differences. This schism affected France, as Catholicism was the predominate religion. It complicated matters that different languages were spoken in the provinces.

The split was caused by three differences in interpretation of biblical scripture: The first issue was – Does the Holy Spirit proceed from the Father or the Son, or the Father and the Son? The Western Church insisted that scripture states that the Holy Spirit proceeds from the Father and the Son. The Church had this doctrine inserted into the Nicene Creed. The relationship between the Father, the Son, and the Holy Ghost is referred to as "filioque."

The second issue that caused the split concerned the question – "Is the pope a leader in the church, or does he have ultimate authority over everyone and everything?" The third issue concerns the number of legitimate Ecumenical Councils that were to be held. Latin-speaking Rome began to assert authority over Greek-speaking Constantinople. Church boundaries and control became issues of dispute.

Latin missionaries from the West rivaled missionaries from the East. Issues such as marriage versus celibacy, rules of fasting, and tonsure (whether the priests should shave the tops of their heads) caused dissension. Patriarch Michael Cerularius and envoys representing Pope St. Leo IX held formal rites of excommunication. They removed each other from their church.

Total alienation came a century and a half later when members of the Fourth Crusade in 1204 captured Constantinople. The Fourth Crusade was originally intended to conquer the Muslims who had gained control of Jerusalem. Deceit, forfeiture of promised compensation, and inherent dislike led to disastrous consequences. What started out as one plan ended up in doing something very different.

The Crusaders led an attack on Constantinople. Thousands of Orthodox Christians were murdered. Churches and icons were desecrated. An undying hostility developed between the Eastern and Western Christians.

There were political issues involved in this massacre. Monies had been promised that were not able to be paid. The Crusaders were cheated of their reward and disgusted at the treachery of the Byzantines. They declared war on Constantinople, which fell to the Crusade on April 4, 1204.

It was the first attack of a Catholic city by a Crusade army. In April 1204, the Crusaders captured and plundered the enormous wealth of

Constantinople. Several Crusaders disagreed with the attack. They left the Crusade to return home.

The Valois Dynasty, the royal house of France from 1328–1589, ruled the kingdom of France during the feudal period until the early Modern Age. This dynasty was active in unifying France. There were thirteen kings of France during this era. In 1348, the pandemic of the Black Death killed one-third of the population of France.

St. Louis of France created a sophisticated administration. He died on the Second Crusade in 1261. The Third Crusade resulted in Richard the Lionheart gaining access to Holy Sites. In 1214, at the Battle of Bouvines, Phillip Augusta defeated John of England, the Flanders Count. The English possessions were reduced to Anjou. This was a great victory for the French Crown.

A succession crisis led to a series of wars known as "The Hundred Years Wars." In 1328, Edward III, King of England, held Charles II of France captive and demanded his ransom. A young peasant girl, who testified that she was guided by visions from Michael, the archangel, requested to be taken to Charles II to help him save France from English domination. Convinced of her purity and devotion, Charles sent seventeen-year-old Joan to the siege of Orleans as part of a relief army.

Nine days after her arrival, the English abandoned the siege. Joan encouraged the French to pursue the English. This brought a second victory to France. Charles II was crowned King of France, with Joan at his side. Joan was later captured by French allies of the English.

She was put on trial by Bishop Cauchon for heresy. The charges against Joan included blasphemy for wearing men's clothing and cutting her hair short in the fashion of men. She refused to admit that her words and deeds violated the rules of the Catholic Church. Joan was found guilty and burned at the stake on May 30, 1431.

She became a national symbol of France. The "Maid of Orleans" was revered as a martyr and canonized as a saint. The victorious conquests of Joan of Arc strengthened French nationalism and the power of the monarch. France changed into an absolute monarchy.

In 1328, Philip of Valois became king of France. His descendants ruled until 1589. In 1630, a Bourbon king gave Valois to his brother, Gaston, duc d'Orleans. Gaston held the duchy (a region owned by a duke or a duchess) until the Revolution of 1790. Valois was dismantled by the redivision of France into regions called departments. What had once been Valois became a region located between Ile de France and Normandy.

The first French colonies were established in 1534. During different times in the history of France, colonies were started around the world – Southern Europe, the Americas, Africa, Oceania, and Antarctica. During the 19th and early 20th century, France built one of the largest colonial empires of all time.

In July 1589, a Dominican monk, Jacques Clement, gained an audience with King Henri III. The monk thrust a long knife into the king's spleen, which eventually killed him. On his deathbed, the Protestant king pleaded with his heir to join the Catholic Church. Henry Navarre became Henry IV of France.

Wars concerning religion began in France in 1562. These wars were fought between French Catholics and Huguenot Protestants. Between two and four million people died from famine, disease, and violence. There were eight conflicts fought between the Catholics and the Protestants during this time in history.

One of the most infamous events was St. Bartholomew's Day Massacre in 1572. Thousands of Protestant Huguenots were killed by Roman Catholics.

The pattern of warfare followed by a period of peace continued until the Edict of Nantes gave the Huguenots protection. These were difficult times for France.

The wars had been fought between the aristocratic House of Bourbon and the House of Guise. The difference in the religious beliefs centered around the presence of Christ in the Holy Eucharist. Did the Eucharist just represent Christ, or was Christ truly present in the wafer? How can this be determined, and by whom?

Amnesty was granted to the Protestants who were involved in these wars, and their civil rights were reinstated. They were also guaranteed the right to "freedom of conscience" in religious matters and the right to bring grievances directly to the king. The Protestants were no longer pressured to leave France. Many Catholic Royalists were willing to serve under Protestant Henry IV's reign. This brought peace and growth to the economy of France. This era was known as "The Golden Age," and Henry IV remains one of France's most beloved kings.

Louis XIV's reign, 1643–1715, was one of the longest in history. Medieval feudalism was eliminated, and France was under the rule of an absolute monarch until the French Revolution and beyond. France was not as large as it is today. Noble families were in charge of their personal properties.

The 15th, 16th, and 17th centuries gave rise to territorial expansion. France became involved in exploration and colonization in Africa and other nations. In the early modern times, to become involved in mercantilism offered many advantages. The height of mercantilism rose under Jean-Baptiste Colbert, the minister of finance for twenty-two years.

To encourage industry, artisans were brought into France. Colbert also decreased barriers to trade. He built an extensive network of roads and canals. He served in his position as Minister of Finance until his death.

One of the most interesting people in the history of France was Marie Antoinette. Although she was born in Austria, she was married at the age of fourteen to the future king of France. She became queen of France in 1774 and ruled until 1793. Some historians refer to her position as being a "pawn on the diplomatic chessboard of Europe." As time passed, the king took a mistress. Marie Antoinette began an affair with Count Axel von Fersen.

An expensive diamond necklace from the jewels belonging to the crown went missing. The necklace was rumored to be a gift from the king to his mistress. A female descendant from the House of Valois, Jeanne de la Monte, had stolen the necklace. She fabricated a plan of deception, using Cardinal Rohan as a means to make money for herself. She began selling the diamonds, one at a time, in London.

Although she was innocent, Marie Antoinette was linked to the theft. She was also accused of loyalties to her homeland, Austria. Marie Antoinette was accused of being a traitor to France. She never got over her mistreatment. Cardinal Rohan was exiled from France. Marie Antoinette's husband was executed, and she was beheaded on the guillotine in 1785.

Political and financial crises created widespread social distress in France in 1787. A shortage of food created dissension among the peasants. The politicians ignored the problems or did not tell the truth about the situation. The Assembly of Notables increased the taxes.

The French Revolution began when an assembly of notables met in February of 1787 to eliminate the budget deficit by raising taxes. This was passed by the Controller of Finances, Charles Alexandre de Calonne. This caused a revolt in the aristocratic parliament. The important courts of justice issued the "Edict of 1788," also known as the "Edict of Versailles" and the "Edict of Tolerance."

The Revolution of 1789 came about because the middle class sought political power. The peasants wanted an improved standard of living. The feudal system had been replaced by wealthy commoners consisting of merchants, manufacturers, and professionals called the "bourgeoisie." France was the most populated country in Europe at the time. This created a great demand for food and consumer goods.

The intellectuals were influenced by the ideas of Voltaire, René Descartes, John Locke, and Benedict de Spinoza. Nine hundred Parisians stormed the Bastille (a former fortress turned into a prison) in an effort to capture gunpowder and two cannons that were known to be stored there. Because he had no orders to do so, De Launay, the officer in charge, refused to hand the gunpowder and cannons over to the raging Parisians. But men had already climbed the walls and entered the Bastille.

The panicking soldiers inside the Bastille started firing at the intruders, and the battle to take over the prison commenced. The Bastille was captured, and the prisoners released. The aristocracy sought allies among the bourgeois and the peasants. Feudalism in France ended at this time in history.

Napoleon Bonaparte was a French military officer and statesman. He led a campaign across Europe during the French Revolution. He was leader of the 1st Consul from 1804–1814. Napoleon crowned himself Emperor of France. He later crowned his brother, Joseph, King of Spain in 1808.

In 1814, Napoleon was defeated and exiled to the island of Elba. He escaped and took control of France. Once again, he became engaged in war. His opponents from the Seventh Coalition defeated him at the Battle of Waterloo. He was exiled on the island of St. Helena in the South Atlantic Ocean. Napoleon died of stomach cancer at the age of 51. The structure in Paris called the Arc de Triomphe began with orders from Napoleon in 1806. It was dedicated to commemorate the soldiers who died in previous wars. This structure is located at the western end of the Champs-Élysées at the center of Place Charles de Gaulle. The Arc is 165 feet tall, which makes it the second-largest triumphal arc ever built.

In 1803, the United States of America negotiated the purchase of the rights to the western half of the Mississippi River Basin from France. Thomas Jefferson sent James Monroe to arrange this purchase. Monroe worked with Napoleon's Minister of Finance, François de Barbé-Marbois. The purchase was made for the price of $27,267,622.00. After disputed boundaries were agreed upon, the states of Louisiana, Missouri, Arkansas, Iowa, North and South Dakota, Nebraska, Oklahoma, Kansas, Colorado, Wyoming, Montana, and Minnesota were included in the purchase.

The world has been blessed by many grand structures found in France.

The Notre-Dame Cathedral is an impressive example of Gothic architecture. It is a medieval Catholic cathedral on an island in the Seine River of France. The cathedral was dedicated to the Virgin Mary. It has enormous rose-colored windows. The cathedral contains three pipe organs and many beautiful church bells.

Construction of the cathedral began in 1163 and was completed in 1200. It has been modified many times through the years. The coronation of Napoleon and the funerals of many kings took place in this cathedral. In 1831, the publication of Victor Hugo's memorable *Hunchback of Notre-Dame* inspired an interest in the cathedral that led to restoration.

Liberation of Paris from German occupation was celebrated in Notre-Dame Cathedral. A fire in April 2019 caused serious damage, forcing the cathedral to be closed for five years. The current Archbishop is Laurent Ulrich. Twelve million people a year visit the Notre-Dame Cathedral of France.

The Eiffel Tower, a famous landmark of Paris, was built in 1887–1889. The tower was designed and built by Gustave Eiffel. This structure is one of the most famous landmarks in the world. The tower is a genius framework of wrought iron imported from Pompeii. Eiffel was one of three engineers who built the Statue of Liberty, a gift from the people of France to the United States of America.

The iron plates for the Eiffel Tower were built in sections in the Eiffel factories. They were taken to the construction site, the sections assembled, and then the tower was erected. The tower stands a majestic 1,083 feet tall. This is the same height as an eighty-story building. It is the tallest structure in Paris. It is the second-tallest free-standing structure in France. In 1991, it was declared a UNESCO World Heritage Site.

The Eiffel Tower is the tallest structure made by humans in the world. The French refer to the tower as "La Dame de Fer" – "The Iron Lady." The tower drew 5,889,000 visitors in 2022. It has elevators for those who cannot climb the height. This author was very fortunate to have stood in the Eiffel Tower and looked down upon Paris during a visit to France.

The Louvre is a national art museum located on the right bank of the Seine River in Paris, France. In 1682, Louis XIV chose the Palace of Versailles as his home place, leaving his old home place, the Louvre, to display the royal collection of *objets d'art.* It was during the French Revolution that the National Assembly decreed that the museum was to be used to display France's vast collection of art.The Louvre Museum officially opened on August 10, 1793, displaying an exhibition of 537 paintings. Today, the Musée du Louvre displays 500,000 objects. Along with the *Mona Lisa* and *Venus de Milo,* you will find sculptures, paintings, drawings, and archaeological artifacts. The Louvre is the largest museum in the world. It has recently received bomb threats.

The Moulin Rouge (Red Mill) was built in 1889 by Charles Zidler and Joseph Oller. It was destroyed in 1915 by fire but was rebuilt. The Moulin Rouge is famous for being the birthplace of the "Can-Can" dance. The Can-Can is depicted in the drawings of renowned artist Toulouse-Lautrec. This seductive dance evolved into an artistic form of its own and helped to create many cabarets across Europe.Charles de Gaulle was a military officer and statesman who led the Free French Forces against Nazi Germany during WWII. He was promoted to the rank of Brigadier General of the Armed Forces. He chaired the Provisional Government from 1944–1946. Charles de Gaulle later became President of the Fifth Republic of France from 1959 to 1969.

The Battle of Dunkirk (Dunkerque) was fought in the area around the French port of Dunkirk during WWII. The German military had forced the British-French allied forces into Belgium, where they were faced with more German military. The Allies were losing the battle. Belgium was lost to the Nazis. The last place to head was the city of Dunkirk, near the only place an evacuation of troops could be attempted.The Germans killed 18,000 French and 3,500 British soldiers, along with 1,000 French civilians. Many of the soldiers and civilians were wounded and fled to the beach in hopes of being rescued. For some unknown reason, Hitler ordered a delay of the offensive plans made to capture Dunkirk. This gave the Allies time to start evacuation efforts. Naval vessels, passenger ferries, yachts, fishing, and pleasure boats joined together in England to carry 338,226 brave men twenty-one miles across the English Channel to safety.

The Americans entered WWII in December 1942. This war was fought against the Allied military forces of Germany, Italy, and Japan. Germany was led by Adolf Hitler, Italy was led by Benito Mussolini, and Japan's

Emperor was Hirohito. U.S. President Franklin D. Roosevelt placed Dwight D. Eisenhower in command of the Allied forces.

On June 17, 1944, in a military strategy called "Operation Overlord," consisting of 326,000 Allies from Great Britain, Canada, the United States of America, and others, commandeered the largest amphibian invasion in history. Around 2,000 African Americans were among the troops that stormed the beaches. A Black medic by the name of Waverly Woodson treated over 200 men. Woodson is credited with saving many lives.

There were more than 50,000 vehicles and 100,000 tons of equipment put on shore. This happened by landing on a fifty-mile stretch of beach in an area of France called Normandy. The different beaches on the coast of Normandy are Omaha Beach, Utah Beach, Sword Beach, Gold Beach, and Juno Beach. There were 5,000 to 12,000 casualties. The number is still changing since it was difficult to find all the bodies. The number of German prisoners captured reached 200,000. This event is known as D-DAY of WWII. The "D" stands for day – the first day of a military invasion. On May 8, 1945, the Allies accepted the surrender of Nazi Germany. Hitler committed suicide.

One of the most interesting places in France is the stream of healing waters in Lourdes. Bernadette Soubirous described an apparition of the Virgin Mary telling her to dig in the earth at Lourdes, and a spring would be found that would bring forth water that would have healing powers. More than 7,000 cases of healing by the water from Lourdes have been reported and documented. The youngest case reported was a two-year-old crippled boy who was healed.

The current president of France is Emmanuel Macron. The Prime Minister of France is Gabriel Attal. The problems in Israel and Palestine have had a negative impact and placed a burden in the hearts of the people of France. Another issue of concern is the European Court of Human Rights, which condemned France for inhuman and degrading human conditions and for a lack of an effective remedy for abusive treatment at Fresnes Prison. The most important concern currently is the financial position of this empire.

France is an old and beautiful nation, rich in history, culture, language, and world-famous landmarks. French cuisine is superb. The people are beautiful, friendly, and helpful to foreigners. This chapter on France has been a joy to research and write about. *Je t'aime. Je t'adore.*

Chapter Twenty-Five:
The Germanic Empire

"They have plundered the world, stripping naked the land in their hunger . . . they slaughter, they seize by false pretenses."

~Tacitus, the Agricola and the Germania

In the times of the Ancient Empires, the Germanic tribes from Scandinavia first settled in what is now modern-day Germany. They are referred to as the Teutonic people. They were a group of people composed of numerous tribes, which centered on the worship of particular cults. These groups of people once occupied central Europe and Scandinavia.

These different ethnic tribes, consisting of the Vandals, Goths, Gepids, and others, migrated from southern Sweden and settled in the mountains north of Transylvania. The tribes shared commonalities of language and a polytheistic religion. This migration occurred in the third century A.D. The Vandals were an ancient Germanic tribe who inhabited what is now southern Poland.

They settled on the banks of the Oder and Vistula Rivers. The Vandals also established kingdoms on the Iberian Peninsula, which consists of Spain and Portugal, in the Mediterranean islands, and North Africa. The name Goth is possibly associated with the Gutones, who lived near the lower Vistula

River in what is now Poland. They were associated with the Wielbark culture, which expanded towards the Black Sea.

This association contributed to the formation of the Chernyakhov culture. Several Gothic groups grew from this association. The Goths formed the Visigoths under King Alaric. They began a long migration that would extend to Spain. This domain lasted until 711 A.D. After this, the Visigoths were absorbed into the Spanish culture.

Along with other tribes, the Gepidae defeated the Huns in Pannonia, a province west of the Danube River. The area in which these tribes settled was called Germania by the Romans. Germania stretched from east to west between the Vistula and Rhine Rivers, and from north to south from Scandinavia to the Danube River. The Germanic people were from the pre-Roman Iron Age – from the sixth to the first centuries B.C.

"To robbery, butchery and rapine, they gave the lying name of government; they create a desolation and call it peace."

~Tacitus, The Agricola and the Germania

Roman Emperor Augustus of the 63–14 B.C. era attempted to conquer a large part of Germania. It was after a lengthy period of wars, known as the Marcomannic Wars, that Germanic groups of people appeared in historical records for the first time. Various groups of Germanic people invaded the Roman Empire and took control of the areas. Eventually, Charlemagne, a Frankish king, became ruler of the Holy Roman Empire.

Chapter Twenty-Six:
The Russian Empire

"I am not yet ready to be Tsar. I know nothing of the business of ruling."

~Tsar Nicholas Romanov II

The decline of rival influences of neighboring powers of the Swedish nation, the Polish-Lithuanian Commonwealth, Persia, and the Ottoman Empire was conducive to the rise of the Russian Empire. This factor also played a role in the 1812–1814 ambitions of Napoleon to conquer Europe.

During its zenith, Russia was one of the largest nations in the world. The 15th century brought the consolidation of the lands around Moscow. Gradually, this consolidation expanded across the continent toward the east coast of the Eurasian landmass. This expansion included such important cities as Novgorod, Minsk, and Kiev.

This consolidation comprised present-day Russia, Belarus, and Ukraine. East Slavic tribes populated the region. The Scandinavian Viking, a Varangian called Prince Rurik, established rule in Novgorod. The Varangians were Swedish conquerors, traders, and settlers. Prince Rurik's descendants ruled in both Kiev and Muscovite Rus until the 17th century.

The territory of Kievan Rus became Orthodox Christian, the official religion of the Byzantine Empire. Remember, the Byzantine Empire was the name of the Eastern Roman Empire. This occurred under the rule of Vladimir the Great. The "Russkaia Pravda," which translates to "Russian Truth," was the first codified law of this ancient kingdom. The Russian kingdom was slowly becoming an empire.

Under the rule of Prince Yaroslav the Wise, many churches were built. These include Saint Sophia in Novgorod and in Kiev. These were inspired by the Hagia Sophia in Constantinople. Christianity served as a unifying political force in Kievan Rus.

After 1132, Kievan Rus became fragmented. This was caused by political dissension within and the decline of its ally, Byzantium. The Mongol army, under the leadership of the Golden Horde commander Batu Khan, invaded Kievan Rus, and in 1240 the kingdom fell. The Mongols dominated the territory until the late 15th century.

Two centuries after the Mongol conquest, the Russian State, ruled by Ivan III, became independent. Russian territories expanded to include Siberia. Between 1721 and 1917, the Russian Empire became one of the largest empires in the world. Catherine the Great was the last empress of Russia.

Catherine ruled from 1772 to 1796. She was able to expand the borders of Russia, bring about judicial and administrative reforms, and acquire a vast art collection that is admired throughout the world. The empress and her husband were known to be mismatched in many ways. They were both believed to have had partners outside the marriage.

The empress corresponded with such notables as Voltaire and Denis Diderot. She wrote operas and children's fairy tales. Catherine also founded the first state-funded school for women. Although she was born a penniless Prussian princess, she was empress of Russia for three decades.

Since the late 1700s, Russia had settlements in North America. These included Alaska, Fort Ross in California, and a number of outposts in Hawaii. In 1867, Russia sold Alaska to the United States. Although this was referred to as "Seward's Folly," it was a most fortunate transaction for the U.S., as Alaska contained many valuable resources.

Abraham Lincoln's Secretary of State, William Seward, was a proponent of territorial expansion. Russian Minister Baron Eduard de Stoeckl came to Washington, D.C., and made contact with Seward. They negotiated and agreed upon the price of $7.2 million for the territory known as Alaska. The official transfer took place on October 18, 1867. Gold and oil were later discovered, which covered the investment cost many times over.

The collapse of the Russian Empire was brought about by the First World War and the Bolshevik Revolution in 1917. Nicholas II, known in the Russian Orthodox Church as Saint Nicholas the Passion-Bearer, was the last Tsar of Russia. He was also the Grand Duke of Finland and King of Congress Poland. He ruled from November 1894 until March 1917, the day he abdicated the throne of Russia when the monarchy was abolished. He and his family were brutally executed by Bolshevik soldiers.

This gave rise to the independence of Poland and Finland. Russia was consolidated into the Soviet Union in 1922. The ruling powers re-incorporated some of the former territories of the Russian Empire. This increased the status of the Soviet Union.

Russia was pagan until the 10th century. In Soviet Russia, all religion was banned. The Russian Orthodox Church has a privileged position and gets to decide which other religions can be officially registered. In the 1990s, a revival in religion caused new churches to be built and old ones to be restored.

Russia has undergone a revival of religion since the beginning of the new millennium. Over 70% of Russians are Orthodox Christians. There are twenty-five million Muslims, 1.5 million Buddhists, and over 179,000 Jewish people living in modern Russia. The Russian Orthodox Church presents itself as the true Russian religion.

Paganism is also popular, as it presents an opportunity for the people to reconnect to their Slavic roots. The Catholic Church and some Protestant denominations have difficulty registering and establishing churches. Only 5% of the population attend church regularly. For the majority of contemporary Russians, religion in Russia seems to be a concern of national identity rather than faith.

This author had the privilege of attending the church service in a Russian Orthodox Church while on two mission trips to Russia. I was very impressed with the older Russian women standing for the long worship service. There were no pews and few chairs to sit on. The women wore babushkas (handkerchiefs) covering their heads. Babushka means grandmother in the Russian language, and Dedushka means grandfather.

Although I do not approve of the Russian government, I love the Russian people. I had the pleasure of going to Russia on a vacation trip, two mission trips, and then a trip with my daughter when she adopted two Russian babies. I have friends in Siberia, and two beautiful adopted granddaughters, Regina (Gina) and Alexandra (Sasha), from an area near Tyumen, Russia, are a joy to my heart.

Chapter Twenty-Seven:
The Spanish Empire

"In all parts of the Old World, as of the New, it was evident that Columbus had kindled a fire in every mariner's heart."

~Charles Kendall Adams

When describing the Spanish Empire, historians are referring to the lands early Spain had dominion over. Spain had overseas territories in the Americas, Africa, the Pacific, and Europe. Fifteenth-century fragmented Spain rivaled Portuguese rule as Spanish explorers set sail in search of trade routes and riches abroad. Later, Spain amassed one of the largest empires in the world.

This new empire covered over seven million square miles of land. Spain and Portugal make up the Iberian Peninsula. The fifteenth-century Iberian Peninsula was home to Christian, Jewish, and Muslim populations. Spain had undergone seven hundred years of war.

The Moors, who were Muslim, had conquered the region in the eighth century. This conquest had forced the Christians to the north of Spain. The Muslims held the stronghold of Granada. The new kingdoms in Spain were not united until King Ferdinand and Queen Isabella were married.

This brought unification of two major realms, Aragon and Castile, under one power. Granada was conquered, and Ferdinand added it to Aragon. The united Spain was anxious to expand and reached across the seas to enhance its power. Christopher Columbus set sail to find a new route to India.

Instead of finding a new route to India, Columbus found a New World. Charles I, through marriage, inherited a long list of titles; Holy Roman Emperor was among his inherited titles. His new empire included the Netherlands, Spain, Austria, and the Holy Roman Empire, along with parts of Italy and overseas colonies.

Philip, son of Charles I, succeeded his father but did not retain rule of the Holy Roman Empire or Austria. Philip became king of Portugal, and the Dutch of the Netherlands gained independence. The flag of the Spanish Empire was the Cross of Burgundy, which was French. Spain had acquired modern-day Belgium, the Netherlands, and Luxembourg.

Flags were flown on the sailing vessels to indicate nationality. Spain's colonization in the New World brought a source of wealth to be channeled into the arts and various technologies. Magellan led an expedition to the New World in 1519, which further increased the revenues of Spain. Spain prospered during the sixteenth and seventeenth centuries.

The high cost of war led to tax hikes in Portugal and Catalonia, causing them to revolt and break off from Spain in 1640. The formidable Spanish Empire existed until the eighteenth century in Europe and the nineteenth century in the Americas. Some Spanish territories gained their independence in the twentieth century. Nearly four hundred million people speak Spanish, and Catholicism is the religion of many of Spain's former conquests in Europe, the Americas, Africa, and Asia.

There are many influences of the Spanish throughout the world. Some of them are: language, using the names of Spanish places for the names of newly established Spanish lands. The Philippines were named after King Philip II. Many of the formerly owned Spanish lands adopted the use of Spanish currency.

What caused the decline of the Spanish Empire? Perhaps it was the overstretching of commitments across the globe. Ruling an empire is a formidable task. Wars are too costly. Decadence in the morals of the culture is a contributing factor. I believe this is a warning to all future empires, including the United States of America.

Sailing from Lisbon in May of 1588, the Spanish Armada was sent to invade England. Philip had hoped to restore Catholicism in England. He was determined to stop Sir Francis Drake's raids against Spanish commerce in the Caribbean in 1585 and 1586. But this did not happen.

Strategies, weather, and lack of experience of the leader were factors that caused the defeat of the Spanish Armada against the English. This saved the English and the Dutch Republic from extinction. The Spanish Empire ruled for over two and one-half centuries. The warships of the Spanish Armada ruled the seas during this time.

Chapter Twenty-Eight:
The British Empire

"The sun never sets on the British Empire."

~The Caledonian Mercury

The above quote was used to describe the mass holdings of the British Empire and meant that the sun was always shining on at least one of its territories. It was during the reign of Elizabeth I in the 1500s that the British Empire had grown to rule over 400 million people. This made Great Britain the largest empire in history. It was composed of colonies, protectorates, dominions, and other territories under the rule of the United Kingdom.

For over a century, the British Empire was the foremost global power. The British legacy impacted the world. Many people speak the English language and have adopted the culture of the British. Britain became the dominant power in the subcontinent of India after its conquest of Mughal Bengal, India's military, in 1757.

Great Britain was the dominant colonial power in North America. The War of Independence resulted in the loss of Britain's oldest and most populated colonies in North America. By 1913, the British Empire was instrumental in ruling over 412 million people. This was over twenty-three percent of the world's population.

The British Empire emerged as the greatest naval power of the nineteenth century. This gave rise to advantages in world trade affairs and increased the prestige and wealth of the United Kingdom. By the twentieth century, Germany began to challenge this economic power. This rivalry caused tensions which led to WWI. The war placed a financial strain on the military and manpower of the British Empire.

By 1920, Great Britain and its colonies covered over twenty-four percent of the earth's total land area. After WWI, Great Britain no longer led the world as the industrial or military power. In WWII, Britain's colonies in East and Southeast Asia were occupied by Japan. Despite Britain's victory over Japan, damage was done to its prestige. This led to the decline of the Crown.

India achieved independence from Britain in 1947. The Suez Canal was a valuable waterway that controlled the passing of ships transporting two-thirds of the oil used in Europe. The canal was nationalized in 1956 by Egyptian President Gamal Abdel Nasser. Nasser was opposed by French and British forces, which were in opposition to the stand of the United States on the operation of the Suez Canal.

There were many conflicting political dynamics surrounding the 120-mile-long man-made waterway. The superpowers were vying for control of this shortcut to the delivery of oil used by Europe. The canal was built under the supervision of French diplomat Ferdinand de Lesseps but was run jointly by a British-French organization.

Middle East politics were an important dynamic, as control of the canal was at stake. Britain's relationship with the Commonwealth nations and the special relationship shared with the United States was threatened. United Nations troops were deployed. Britain's Prime Minister, Anthony Eden, resigned as its status as a declining empire was emphasized.

The United Nations threatened Britain with sanctions if there were any casualties from aerial bombing of targets. Soviet leader Nikita Khrushchev accused the Crown of "British Imperialism" and threatened to send nuclear missiles against Western Europe if the tri-partisan Israeli-French-British military forces did not withdraw. U.S. President Eisenhower intervened with warnings that a worldwide catastrophe would result from reckless interference. These pressuring dynamics dragged the North Atlantic Treaty Organization (NATO) into the conflict.

The Soviet intervention on the side of Egypt increased friendly relations with the Arabs. U.S. President Eisenhower threatened all three nations with economic sanctions if the attack on the canal was not ended. The threats were effective, and all three nations withdrew. The Suez Canal was reopened in March 1957.

The Suez Canal was a pivotal Cold War event among the superpowers of the world. The canal crisis involved three major religions—Jewish, Muslim, and Christian—in an international situation that could possibly bring on a nuclear war that would result in the end of time. Egypt was victorious, and most supporting troops were withdrawn by late 1956 and early 1957. Resentments festered because the U.S. did not fund the Aswan Dam project and opposed the British on the Suez Canal project. India received its independence in 1947. Britain granted independence to most of its territories.

On July 1, 1997, Britain transferred Hong Kong to China. This marked the end of the British Empire. Fourteen overseas territories remain under British rule. Many joined the Commonwealth Nations. Several of these retain the common monarch of England, which is Charles III.

Chapter Twenty-Nine:
The Empire of Australia - The Land Down Under

"Australia is a nation of compassion. Courage, and compassion, and a third of these great values: resilience."

~Kevin Rudd

Many, many years ago during the Cretaceous period, Antarctica and Australia separated from Gondwana, a supercontinent. Near the end of the Paleocene Epoch, Australia had separated from Antarctica. Papua New Guinea and Tasmania were cut off from mainland Australia as the ice melted over a period of 6,000 years. Australia is surrounded by the Indian Ocean, the Pacific Ocean, and the Southern Ocean.

The geographical regions that make up large land masses in the world are known as the seven continents – Asia, Africa, North America, South America, Antarctica, Europe, and Australia. In terms of land area, Australia is the smallest continent. The continent is divided into smaller regions. This division serves several purposes.

Migration of people occurred over the land bridge and short water crossings from Asia between the continents. The Aborigine natives of Australia occupied mainland Australia some 50,000 to 65,000 years ago.

The Aborigines are one of the oldest living populations in existence. Indigenous people make up 2.4% of the population in the "Land Down Under."

There were many groups of Aborigines that were defined by language and cultural traditions. These hunters and gatherers consisted of about 600 tribes. The tribes found refuge in caves or built semi-permanent rock structures for shelter. The Madjedbebe rock shelter in Arnhem Land, situated in the north of the continent, provides archaeological evidence of the oldest human settlement in Australia.

The Aborigines adapted to many challenges such as diverse environments, changing climates, and predatory animals. One of the rituals that developed in the culture was the passing of stories from one generation to the next. The Aborigines had a "story" about their ancestor's spirit to pass on to their descendants. This phenomenon is referred to as Tjukurpa or "Dreamtime." In some Aboriginal communities, the spirit who made the world is called Wanadjina.

The Dreamtime philosophy suggests that the spirit of Aboriginal ancestors created the world from a void. These ancestral spirits lived in water holes, streams, rivers, rocks, mountains, and the sky. They also inhabit plants, animals, and humans. The wind, rain, thunder, and lightning – everything had a spirit. Some stories reveal that ancestral spirits sometimes take the form of a large snake. Each tribe of Aborigines was given a totem and land to live on; each person was also given a Dreamtime story.

Designated sites were revealed as sacred places. The indigenous Aborigine considered Dreamtime a beginning that never ended. This concept covered the past, present, and the future. The spirits dictate the laws of the land and how individuals are to live and behave toward one another. Ritual ceremonies for birth, marriage, and death – all significant rites of passage – are revealed by the spirits and encouraged to be honored by the Aborigines.

The Aborigine ritual ceremonies include initiations, songs, and dances that are designed to please the spirits of their ancestors. Dreamtime beliefs support the concept that the spirits have the ability to change into animals and other forms such as the Rainbow Serpent. All of the spirit forms are to watch over the people. The phenomena of Dreamtime are unquestionably believed in the world of the Australian Aborigine.

Lake Mungo in this new land, which dates as far back as 41,000 years ago, provides evidence of a site that has religious implications of cremation ceremonies. Madjedbebe, a rock shelter, contains evidence of the world's oldest ground-edge axes, flints, and ochre – a natural clay pigment used for body painting and pictorial messages that tell a Dreamtime story. There is evidence that the mineral mica was used to enhance Aboriginal art. The Aboriginal art depicts drawings of large snakes, boomerangs, mountains, and animals.

The life of the Aborigine was interrupted by the exploration of outsiders. In 1606, William Janszoon, representing the Dutch East India Company, arrived in what is present-day Cape York, Queensland. Janszoon met with the Aboriginal people. He explored the southern areas of the new land. The newly discovered land was first called New Holland.

In 1642, Abel Tasman led the first known European expedition to reach Van Diemen's Land. The island was later called Tasmania. Tasman mapped the area, studied, and made notes about the natives. He also explored the area called New Guinea. The capital of Tasmania is Hobart.

The most well-known expedition was that of James Cook. In 1770, Cook claimed the land known as New Holland for Great Britain. The name was changed to New South Wales. The tract of land known as New South Wales was larger than the whole of Europe. After Cook's death, John Harris, in the *Voyages and Travel* magazine, recommended sending convicts to Botany Bay, which is in Sydney, New South Wales. The first fleet carrying convicts arrived in Botany Bay in January 1778; the first penal colony was established at this time.

At times, a convict served part of the court sentence in a British prison and then was given a "conditional pardon" if he/she agreed to finish the sentence in New South Wales. The New South Wales records listed the convicts as servants, laborers, plowmen, shoemakers, stockmen, wives, grooms, and shepherds. Within five years, eighty-five percent of the convicts were emancipated. The newly emancipated individual could qualify for a land grant. This meant that for most of their lives, those who were once convicts were now free to earn good wages. Samuel Terry was an ex-convict who became Australia's wealthiest citizen.

Women were among forty percent of those indicted and sent to prison. Men and boys made up the bulk of Australia's penal colonies. A family was thought of as a man and a woman and any children that might come from that arrangement. Homosexuality was not considered. Only a few White men married Aboriginal women. The children from these relationships were called half-castes.

A penal colony was established on Norfolk Island. In time, a colony for convicts was also placed in Tasmania. The penal colony was a place where convicts were brought from Great Britain and placed in situations where they were forced to work off the sentence they were given by the court. Many of the convicts later became respected citizens of New South Wales.

In 1789, Sir Joseph Banks, along with an American, James Matra, suggested that Australia would be suitable for plantations – sugar, cotton, tobacco, timber, and flax. This plan would benefit the economy of Australia and the convicts. It would place the penal colony in a position to be involved in commerce and trade. This would also enhance the image of Australia in the world.

Because the Aborigines were isolated from the world, they had no natural resistance to disease. An outbreak of smallpox occurred in April 1789. This epidemic killed about one-half of the Aborigines. The epidemic had probably been spread by settlers.

Other diseases such as measles, influenza, typhoid, and tuberculosis resulted in a large death count of the Aborigines. The number of indigenous Australians decreased drastically. Venereal disease reduced fertility rates, which resulted in fewer childbirths.

In 1801, Matthew Flinders led the first circumnavigation of the continent and suggested the name of "Australia" for the unknown South Land. An Aborigine by the name of Bungaree accompanied Flinders and was the first person born on the continent to circumnavigate it. In 1820, Sir Thomas Brisbane commissioned Hamilton Hume and Captain William Hovell to find new grazing lands in the south of the colony. They found good agricultural and grazing lands between Gunning, Australia, and Corio Bay, Port Phillip. Many locations, such as rivers that were found, retain their Aboriginal names. These include the Avoca River, Belyando River, and the Cogoon River.

Major Edmund Lockyer established a settlement on King George Sound in 1826. Count Paul Edmond Strzelecki, a Polish mountain climber, became the first European to ascend the Australian Alps' highest peak, which he named Mt. Kosciuszko in 1839.

In the 1840s, Roderick Murchison, a Scottish geologist, predicted that Australia had economically significant deposits of gold. This was proven by prospectors and diggers. A mineralogist, William Smith, sent his first gold sample to Murchison hoping to receive money for his exploration expenses. News of Smith's successful finding of gold traveled fast.

In May 1851, Edward Hargrave and a few other prospectors announced that they had struck gold. This announcement attracted people with a variety of skills and professions to settle in Australia. This helped to create a thriving economy. It also resulted in convict colonies becoming progressive cities. In 1869, the world's largest gold nugget was found by John Deeson and Richard Oates.

Hargrave and his team first found flecks of gold and then gold nuggets in Lewis Ponds Creek. Gold was found in northern Queensland in the 1860s. It was also found in the Pilbara regions of Western Australia. The Pilbara discovery was in the 1880s. James Regan and John Dunlop discovered gold in Ballarat at Poverty Point; this discovery became the most productive alluvial (found in a stream) gold field at that time.

The colony's major export was agriculture. Governmental officials attempted to suppress the news of the gold discovery in order to prevent a sudden loss of agricultural workers. The loss of agricultural workers would upset the economy. But the news of the gold discovery leaked out to the rest of the world.

In the late 1800s, John McDouall Stuart mapped out the route which led to the Australian Overland Telegraph Line. The final contract to build the line was secured in 1870. This system was 2,000 miles long. It was constructed to send messages from Darwin to Adelaide, the capital of South Australia.

This system allowed communication from Australia with the rest of the world. When the Overland Telegraph Line was linked to a submarine telegraph cable, the communication time with Europe decreased from months to hours. Australia was no longer isolated from the world. This had an impact on all facets of life in the Land Down Under.

Afghans, who were cameleers (camel drivers), were shipped into Australia with their camels at intervals of three years from 1869 to 1930. Camel trains carted woolen bales from the Outback sheep stations to the marketplace or places where the bales could be shipped out and sold. The climate was too harsh for horses. The camel transport system provided a link between the coastal cities and the remote cattle and sheep grazing stations.

The majority of the camel drivers were Muslim. This established Islam in Australia. The country's first mosque was built in Marree, in South Australia, in 1861. A mosque was also built in Adelaide. Several mosques were later built in Western Australia.

In 1869, part-white children of Aborigines were removed from their tribe and placed in orphanages. This was done by Australian state government agencies. Half-caste Aboriginal children up to age sixteen had guardians to oversee their circumstances. The guardians made decisions on where the children would live and work.

In the 1900s, the former colonies were influenced by voters to form one national government – the Federation. One of the first decisions of the new government was to give women the right to vote. The First Nations women (Aborigines) did not get the right to vote until 1962. The White Australian

Policy, also known as the Immigration Restriction Act of 1901, limited the ethnicity of those who wished to migrate to Australia. This was an attempt to keep the population British. Australia gained partial independence from the United Kingdom on January 1, 1901, but did not have full independence until the Australia Act of 1986.

In 1903, the bush ballad, "Waltzing Matilda," made its debut. This ballad has been described as Australia's unofficial national anthem. The term "waltzing" is Australian slang for traveling on foot. When traveling on foot, one carries his belongings in a sack across his back called a "Matilda."

The song describes the happenings of an itinerant worker who is called a "swagman" while cooking a stolen jumbuck (sheep) over a bush campfire. Three mounted policemen show up to arrest the swagman. The swagman told the policeman, "You'll never catch me alive." He then committed suicide by drowning himself in a billabong (waterhole). Forever after, the man's ghost haunted the site.

In 1904, the parliament sought ways to settle disputes between workers and employers. The Commonwealth Court of Conciliation and Arbitration was set in place. In 1908, the Harvester judgment made a landmark decision that wage rates had to be fair and reasonable. The first pensions for the elderly and invalids were introduced. The reconstruction of Aboriginal languages was also revived at this time.

In early 1914, the political assassination of an heir to a European throne increased tensions between the mighty empires of Europe. World War I commenced. As a dominion of the British Empire, Australia willingly joined the war on the side of Great Britain. On August 4, 1914, Britain and Australia joined WWI. Around 410,000 people enlisted to serve in Australia's armed forces.

Over 330,000 Australian soldiers and nurses served in overseas military campaigns. In 1915, some 30,000 Australians and New Zealanders served on the Gallipoli Peninsula, southwest of Constantinople. Efforts were made by allied troops to capture the peninsula and assist naval operations that would open up the Dardanelle Straits for an allied attack on the enemy. Over 8,700 AIF (Australian Imperial Force) soldiers lost their lives, and 18,000 were wounded. Evacuation of the wounded was a success.

In 1916, a large part of the AIF from Gallipoli transferred to France to serve on the Western Front. This ended up creating a loss of 46,000 troops. Over 330,000 Australian soldiers and nurses served overseas in military campaigns during WWI. Australia gained international recognition for the bravery of its men and women who served in this war.

In 1921, Edith Cowan was the first woman elected to the Australian Assembly Committee. It was at this time in Australia's development that Sydney got electricity. It was also the time of the Great Depression. The 1929 Depression had a great impact on Australia. Thirty percent of the population were unemployed. The people had backyard gardens to help provide food. It took Australia ten years to recover from the Depression.

In 1938, a National Day of Mourning was established to recognize the discrimination of the First Nation people (the Aborigines). This recognition was to validate the rights of the Aborigines to be given land and economic considerations. The First Nation people were also to be included in the census. Australians were to be assessed on their skills and abilities and not on race or nationality.

On September 3, 1939, Australia entered World War II. They fought with Great Britain and America against Germany, Italy, and Japan. The Australians felt connected to America through Great Britain. They fought in the European theater, North African campaign, and the South Pacific theater.

Australia came under direct attack for the first time in its post-colonial history. The largest surrender in British history occurred in Singapore just four days before Australia was attacked.

In March 1942, U.S. President Franklin Roosevelt formulated a defense plan with Australia. Roosevelt had appointed General MacArthur as supreme commander of the South Pacific. This created a shift in Australia's foreign policy. MacArthur moved his headquarters to Melbourne in 1942. On June 8, 1942, Japan shelled Sydney's suburbs and the city of Newcastle. The shelling by the Japanese mini-subs did minimal damage. The main impact was planting the possibility of a future invasion in the minds of the people.

On February 9, 1942, two hundred and forty-two Japanese aircraft bombed Darwin, Australia. Most of the people left the city hoping to find a safer place. Two hundred thirty-five people were killed, and many were wounded. The Japanese aircrews targeted the civil infrastructure, sank eight ships, and destroyed twenty military aircraft. This prevented the allies from using the facilities. There were more than 100 air raids on Australia during 1942–1943.

The RAAF (Royal Australian Air Force) actively defended Great Britain. Many Australians were active in the victory at Attapan in the Mediterranean Sea. Australia suffered losses in Greece, Crete, and when Rommel scored his triumphs in North Africa. The RAAF and supporting ground troops were successful in the siege of Tobruk, near the border of Egypt.

Some 30,000 Australians died in WWII. There were 65,000 Australians injured in the campaigns throughout the world. More than 30,000 became prisoners of war between 1940 and 1945. The endurance, courage, and "mateship" philosophy depict the character and indomitable spirit of the Australian identity.

Following WWII, Australia launched a massive immigration program. The idea was "to populate or perish." For the first time, Jews migrated to Australia. More than two million people migrated from Europe within twenty years after the war ended.

The intention was to lure the bulk of immigrants from the British Isles. The hope was to preserve the British character of Australian society. Immigrants came from Greece, Italy, Malta, Germany, Yugoslavia, and the Netherlands. The immigrants were assured that employment could be found.

The construction of sixteen major dams and seven power stations created the largest engineering project Australia had ever undertaken. The project required hiring over 100,000 people. The newly hired people came from thirty nations around the world. This resulted in establishing a multicultural atmosphere in Australia. The project was called the Snowy Mountain Scheme. It was constructed between 1949 and 1974.

In the political arena, the Liberal Party of Australia was established in the late 1940s. The platform of the political activists was to work for social justice, liberty, national power, progress, and the full development of the individual citizen. Prime Minister John Curtin and Attorney General H.V. Evatt headed up a delegation to discuss the formation of the United Nations. Australia played a significant role in the early years of the organization. H.V. Evatt was elected president of the third session of the United Nations General Assembly.

Religious beliefs of the Australians were influenced by the Church of England, which held a position of privilege in early colonial Australia. The Church Act of 1836, drafted by John Plunkett, established legal equality for Anglicans, Catholics, Presbyterians, Congregationalists, Baptists, and

Lutherans to set up churches in the 19th century. Irish Catholics were transported to Australia through the British Criminal Justice system when the penal colonies were established. By 1821, Australian society was Anglo-Celtic. The first census in 1911 showed 96% of Australians identified themselves as Christian.

In 1929, the first Catholic, James Scullin, was chosen as Prime Minister (the Prime Minister is the highest ruling leader in Australia). An Australian Jew, Isaac Isaacs, was appointed governor-general in 1930. A space was provided on the census form to declare "no religion." The number of respondents declaring "no religion" has increased to 38.9% in the 2021 census.

Weekly attendance of church worship services has dropped to 4% of the population. Christian denomination membership has decreased over a period of fifteen years from 63.9% to 43.9%. There has been a steady decline of Australians who declare an affiliation with Christianity. This is a definite sign that there is trouble in Paradise. This causes me great concern. Are Australians turning away from God?

As author, my purpose in writing this book is to furnish evidence that the children of God are turning away from Him, the Commandments He gave Moses, and the dictates He has provided in His Word – the Holy Bible. Satan is keeping God's heirs involved in busy work and luring us into ungodly activities. My purpose in presenting religious, historical, geographical, political, and biographical information is to encourage all who read this book to consider II Chronicles 7:14 as a map for the soul:

"If my people who are called by name will humble themselves, and pray and seek my face and turn from their wicked ways, then will I hear from heaven and will forgive their sin and heal their land."

The churches in Australia with the largest number of members are the Catholic, the Anglican, and the Uniting Church of Australia. Catholic school enrollment numbers are second to government schools. There are two Catholic universities in Australia. Christian charity organizations, including St. Vincent de Paul Society, Salvation Army, Anglicare, and Youth Off the Streets, have national support.

Notable Australian Christians include Mary MacKillop, founder of the Sisters of Saint Joseph of the Sacred Heart. She was from Melbourne. Mary was educated in private Catholic schools and by her scholarly father. She worked as a governess but later started her own boarding school.

Mary was involved in maintaining an orphanage and in establishing a home for the aged. She formed a group known as "The Josephite Sisters." This group followed and provided care for workers, farmers, and miners traveling to the outback. The number of workers in the Josephite Sisters group expanded to 130. They worked in forty charitable organizations across Australia.

Another notable Christian worker was Reverend Doctor John Flynn. He established "The Royal Flying Doctor Service" of Australia in 1928. This is a non-profit organization that provides health care to people who live in remote areas. They fly to the distant outback regions of Australia.

Doctor John Flynn's work was the impetus for the establishment of the Australian Inland Mission. He formed the Area Medical Service in Cloncurry, Queensland. This became "The Royal Flying Doctor Service." This Christian organization is still providing medical services to Australians in remote areas at the present time.

A First Nation Aborigine from the Yorta tribe by the name of Douglas Ralph Nicholl was a very talented man. He established his reputation as an athlete while attending secondary school and the university. He won medals in Australian football, sprinting, boxing, and boomerang throwing competitions. He was also an excellent speaker.

When he was eight years old, Douglas witnessed the kidnapping of his sister, who was placed in Cootamundra, a home for Aborigine girls. She was trained as domestic help. Along with his father, Douglas worked on sheep stations. He joined the Church of Christ in 1932.

During his service in WWII, Douglas was a boomerang thrower. He trained others to be proficient in this skill. Although the Aborigines used the boomerang to kill animals for food, it can be a lethal weapon to be used on humans. Douglas was highly skilled in his abilities with the boomerang.

The boomerang is representative of the Australian Aborigine culture. The Aborigines used the boomerang as a hunting weapon and in competitive sports events. The boomerang was a symbol of endurance. It is considered as old as the continent. The original boomerangs were thought to have been made of bone. The boomerang links the Aborigines to their long presence in The Land Down Under. After the war, this First Nation native, Douglas Nicholl, became an activist in the rights of the Aborigines. He made speeches wherever he could, supporting Aborigine land ownership and any law that gave them equal privileges to Whites. Because he was known for his athletic accomplishments, he was welcomed in Australian society. He became famous and was knighted as Sir Douglas Nicholl in 1972. He learned to interact with the media. He became the first non-white governor of Australia. In 1922, his portrait was placed on an Australian postage stamp.

In the 1950s, allegations of Communist activities in government mounted. Seventeen thousand Australians served in the Korean Conflict. There were more than 1,500 casualties. Three hundred and thirty-nine Australians were killed. In 1954, Australia had its first visit from a reigning monarch, Queen Elizabeth II.

In 1956, television made its debut in Australia. In that same year, Melbourne hosted the Olympics. Australia enjoyed its first international music chart hit— "A Pub with No Beer" by Slim Dusty. British and

Hollywood movie studios started producing epics about Australian history, some featuring Chip Rafferty and some starring Peter Finch.

During the 1960s, Australian conscripts were sent to Vietnam to support efforts against Communism. In 1966, U.S. President Lyndon Johnson brought out large street gatherings to greet him as the first American president to visit Australia. In 1972, Gough Whitlam led the Australian Party to withdraw troops from Vietnam. He also addressed higher education fees and established a free health care system. Whitlam also furthered the program of rights for the Aborigines.

Queen Elizabeth II officially opened the Sydney Opera House on October 20, 1973. Jorn Utzon designed the original structure. Peter Hall was head of the architectural team. The building and its surroundings occupy the area of Bennelong Point in Sydney Harbor.

The Sydney Opera House is a multi-venue performing arts center. More than 1,500 performances a year are held there. Approximately 1.2 million attendees enjoy these performances. Each year the site is visited by eight million people. An agency of the New South Wales government manages the Sydney Opera House Trust.

In 1986, Australia produced the movie "The Man from Snowy River," starring Hollywood actor Kirk Douglas. This Australian story was taken from the poem of the same title by Australian Banjo Patterson, a poet and writer. The plot of the story informs the viewer that the father of the protagonist, Jim Craig, was killed. Jim believed it was necessary for him to go to the Australian lowlands to seek work to save the land he and his father had been living on. Jim finds work on a ranch that breeds racing horses. Jim falls in love with the owner's daughter, Jessica. Watch this old movie to find out what happens.

By 1991, Australia was in recession mode as a result of domestic governmental policies. Unemployment was high. Hundreds of farmers were forced off the land. Land management in the form of conservation and agricultural purposes provided the farmers useful information such as statistics and other data.

The names of the land boundaries of the regions often overlap. Australia is divided into states and territories. There is the Northern Territory, Australian Capital Territory, Western Australia, Tasmania, and New South Wales. The six states are Queensland, New South Wales, South Australia, Tasmania, Victoria, and Western Australia.

The states and territories are divided into electoral regions for political purposes. Australia is the sixth-largest country in the world. Urban cities are defined as having 1,000 or more people. Local governmental areas are referred to as cities, councils, shires, or towns. The largest city in Australia is Sydney, which is often mistaken as the capital.

Fantastic beaches are found in Sydney. The Blue Mountains are also found in Sydney. The Sydney Opera House offers a multi-venue performing arts center. The best time to visit Sydney is September through November and March through May.

The Great Barrier Reef in Australia is the world's largest coral reef collection. It contains 2,900 individual coral reefs. The reef is off the coast of Queensland in Northeast Australia. The Great Barrier Reef is the largest natural structure on Earth. It can be seen from outer space.

The reef extends for 1,250 miles. The width of the reef ranges from 37 to 150 miles in some areas. The total group of reefs covers 133,000 square miles. There are over 1,600 species of fish found on the reef. Six of the world's seven species of marine turtles make the Great Barrier Reef home.

In 1977, it was listed as one of the seven natural wonders of the world. In 2006, the Queensland National Trust named the Great Barrier Reef a state icon. Tourism revenues generate three billion dollars per year to help cover the costs associated with the welfare of the reef. The Great Barrier Reef is one of the major tourist attractions in Australia. It was placed on Australia's World Heritage Sites List in 2007. Every five years, the Great Reef Marine Park Act of 1975 issues a report on the health of the reef, unwanted pressures, and future considerations.

There are many interesting creatures found in Australia. The koala is a herbivorous marsupial native to Australia. The closest living relative of the koala is the wombat. The koala, a cuddly-appearing creature, is found mostly in coastal areas in eastern and southern regions, around Queensland and in New South Wales and Victoria.

The physical markings of the koala are characterized by a body length of 24–30 inches and a varying weight of 8–33 pounds. The color of the koala varies from silver-gray to chocolate brown. The koala features a stout, tailless body with a large head that has fluffy ears and a large, dark nose. Adult males make a bellowing noise that intimidates rivals and attracts mates. The males mark their presence with secretions from their scent glands.

The diet of the koala consists mostly of eucalyptus leaves. They sleep 15–20 hours a day. The koalas are asocial, only bonding with the mother. Young koalas, along with baby kangaroos, are known as "joeys."

The koalas have few predators. They are, however, threatened by the pathogen Chalmydiacea and a koala neurovirus. Other threats include habitat destruction, bushfires, and droughts. Urbanization, which limits the building of habitats, is also a threat to the koala.

The animal that Australia is most associated with is the kangaroo. According to the government, there are approximately thirty-four million kangaroos in Australia. Kangaroos have powerful hind legs with large feet. The red kangaroo can reach a height of six feet. The tails are large and are used for balancing. Kangaroos are shot for meat consumption as they are thought to offer low levels of fat.

The name kangaroo originally came from the expression "Guugu Yimithirr," which means "I don't know" or "I don't understand." Locally, kangaroos are referred to as "roos." They travel in groups known as "mobs." Male "roos" are called bucks, boomers, jacks, or old men. The female kangaroo is called a doe, a flyer, or a jill. Wallabies are a smaller version of the kangaroo.

The female kangaroo has a pouch called a marsupium. The infants, called joeys, complete their postnatal development in this pouch. The kangaroo has special teeth features uncommon to other mammals. The incisors are able to crop the grass next to the ground.

The molars chop and grind up the grass. The silica in the grass wears the molars down, and they eventually fall out. They are replaced by new teeth. This process also occurs in elephants and manatees.

The kangaroo appears on the Australian Coat of Arms. Kangaroo logos represent Australia in the business world and the culture. Qantas Airlines is an example of this feature. Some Australian currency also features the kangaroo logo. Another Australian logo is the boomerang.

Continuing with interesting creatures indigenous to or found in Australia, the bandicoot is an omnivorous marsupial endemic to the New Guinea region. They are usually about 12–31 inches long. Bandicoots look like a large rat. There are around twenty species of bandicoots.

The ostrich, which is native to Africa, is found in small numbers in Australia. The emu, smaller than the ostrich, is native to Australia. Emus feed on plants and insects but can go weeks without eating. The female can lay several clutches of eggs, but the male incubates the eggs.

The platypuses are found only in Tasmania and Australia. They are the only mammals to lay eggs. They are semi-aquatic and can be found in rivers and streams. They use electrosensors to find their prey. The predators of the platypus are snakes, owls, and hawks. They can survive in captivity for many years.

The Australian dingo dogs migrated from Asia. The dingo dog is a medium-sized canine capable of great speed, agility, and stamina. This animal was once domesticated and was probably brought to Australia along with Asians on expedition trips. Fossils were found that suggest that dingoes were first found in Australia 4,000 years ago.

Dingoes are one of Australia's most feared predators. They have converted into a wild state for hundreds of years. They live away from humans. It is against the law to feed dingoes. There are stories of dingoes dragging young children away from camps. Many children were never found.

The cassowary bird is a flightless bird native to the tropical regions and forests of northeastern Australia, New Zealand, New Guinea, and Indonesia. The female is larger and brighter than the male. Females can be found that reach a height of 6'6" and weigh as much as 130 pounds. The cassowaries are wary of humans, but if provoked, they can inflict serious or fatal injuries.

The wombats are stout, muscular marsupials that are native to Australia. They look like a cross between a bear, pig, and gopher. They eat grass, fruit, shrub roots, and fungi. They can grow up to 40 inches long and weigh as much as 77 pounds. They are burrowing animals. The lifespan of a wombat is 5–7 years.

One of the most unique animals found only on the island of Tasmania is the "Tasmanian Devil." Although only the size of a small dog, the devil is the largest carnivorous marsupial in the world. The physical characteristics of the devil include the following: (1) stocky, muscular build, (2) black fur with white patches on the chest and rump, (3) pungent odor, (4) their loud, screeching noise, and (5) going into a frenzy when eating.

The devils are communal while eating and defecating. They are surprisingly fast, can climb trees, and swim across rivers. The males will fight over females. The females ovulate three times during mating season. Eighty percent of the females are observed to be pregnant during the annual mating season.

The gestation period is only three weeks. Females can give birth to twenty to thirty young during their lifespan. There are only four nipples in the pouch. Few newborns survive because competition is fierce. In 2008, the devils were declared an endangered species.

Crocodiles are found in Africa, Asia, the Americas, and Australia. The Australian crocodiles are found in both freshwater and saltwater. Crocodile attacks are common and real in Australia. In 2023, a man disappeared in the northern part of Queensland. The police suspected crocodile activity, so they captured and euthanized two suspiciously large crocs and found remains believed to have belonged to the missing man. Crocodile management plans are in place to protect humans.

The diet of the crocodile consists of fish, birds, mammals, and sometimes sharks. Kakadu National Park is the best place to see crocodiles in Australia. Hunting for crocodiles has been banned in Australia since 1971.

Modern Australia is a highly developed country with a high-income economy. It ranks as the world's thirteenth-largest economy, with the tenth-highest per capita income and the eighth-highest human development ranking index. Life expectancy is also high in Australia. Education levels reach top levels in this nation. Australia has a world reputation for democratic freedoms, available health care policies, civil liberties, and political rights.

Chapter Thirty:
The Austria-Hungarian Empire

"I am the last ruler of the Old World."

~Franz Joseph, Emperor

In 1273 AD, a Hapsburg, Rudolph I, was elected as Holy Roman Emperor. A member of the Hapsburg dynasty held the position of king of Spain from 1516 until 1700. They often married second- and third-degree cousins. The family held the title until the dissolution of the Holy Roman Empire in 1806. The extended family members were involved in the formation of the Austria-Hungarian Empire.

The Austria-Hungarian Kingdom consisted of two countries during the era of 1867–1918. The two countries were located in central Europe. The capital of Austria was Vienna, and the capital of Hungary was Budapest. One nation had a king, and the other had an emperor. The Hapsburg Dynasty was the ruling faction for 600 years.

During the nineteenth century, the empire began to expand its capitalist institutions such as banking, industry, and manufacturing. Franz Joseph was emperor of Austria from 1848 to 1916 and king of Hungary from 1869 to 1916. He divided the empire into a dual monarchy. The Hapsburgs were a prominent family of the Holy Roman Empire.

By the mid-1800s, Prussia became a rival of Austria as an influential German state. The king of Hungary died and left no heir during a battle against the Ottomans; the crown passed to his brother-in-law, a Hapsburg. An attempt was made by the Ottomans to take Vienna but failed, and the Ottomans were beaten by the Austrians. The Austria-Hungarian Empire was instrumental in the political influences that led to WWI.

Although the Austria-Hungarian Empire was a large empire, the leaders had not acquired overseas colonies like other major European powers. The spark that started WWI was the assassination of Franz Ferdinand. A Serb nationalist shot the archduke on June 28, 1914, in Sarajevo, a territory of Bosnia. All of Europe was involved in war within a month.

Many states that belonged to the Austria-Hungarian Empire claimed their independence, and by 1919, the Austria-Hungarian Empire ceased to exist. The Ottoman and the Austria-Hungarian Empires were broken into smaller states after WWI. These newly created states included Serbia, Bosnia, Croatia, Slovenia, Czechoslovakia, and Poland. Some territories were given to Italy and Romania.

Chapter Thirty-One:
The Empire of Modern Germany

"Germany has become a country that many people abroad associate with hope."

~Angels Merkel

The unification of disassociated states ruled by kings, princes, and dukes who had little more than a common language and similar cultural values resulted in the rise of the Modern German Empire. The formation of this empire gradually developed during the time frame between 1866 and January 1871. Leaders of the German-speaking states decided to unite with Prussia to form a German nation. The formation of the nation of Germany into the German Empire was formally announced on January 18, 1871.

The latter empires include the Austria-Hungarian Empire, the Romanov Dynasty of Russia, and continue on to Bismarck relinquishing power as the Second Reich of Germany came under the influence of Adolf Hitler in the early part of the 1930s. The modern German Empire, also referred to as Imperial Germany and later called the Third Reich, is considered to have come into existence in the early 1800s. The North German state of Prussia had been involved in three short but successful wars. The leading factions of the Danish Province, the Hapsburg Monarchy, and France had been conquered.

The Roman Empire was called "The First Reich." "Reich" is the German word for "Empire." Diplomats, the ruling cabinet members, and the hereditary rulers of the areas of Bavaria, Baden, Wittenberg, and Hesse-Darmstadt were the dominant powers in early modern Germany. On January 30, 1933, Adolf Hitler was appointed Chancellor of Germany.

Rearmament of Germany was initiated immediately. Hitler transformed Germany into a totalitarian dictatorship. He claimed that the Third Reich was the successor of the Holy Roman Empire. Hitler began to eliminate political opposition. He consolidated powers to carry out his plans. In 1934, a German referendum confirmed Adolf Hitler as Führer (leader). His word became the law.

In spite of being in the midst of a worldwide economic depression, the Nazi Party restored economic stability and ended unemployment. Hitler's administration undertook extensive public works projects. Germany built an extensive autobahn – a massive motorway. Hitler brought Germany out of a recession.

Adolf Hitler had a perverted view of some of the ideas of scientists and philosophers. This included his view on eugenics. Eugenics was proposed by Sir Francis Galton, who suggested that the human race could be improved by "arranging reproduction." Hitler believed that the German people were a "master race" – the purest branch of the Aryan race. He advocated a belief in antisemitism. German Jews made up less than one percent of the German population.

Jews, Slavs, homosexuals, liberals, communists, Jehovah's Witnesses, Freemasons, and those who refused to work were deported, imprisoned, or murdered. Genocide, mass murder, and forced labor policies were carried out. Implementation of these policies resulted in the "Holocaust." The term Holocaust is a Greek word meaning "burnt offering." Many Jews were sterilized, and unwanted abortions were performed on women.

Nazi Germany murdered six million Jews across German-occupied Europe. Mass shootings and poisonous gassings were carried out in extermination camps such as Auschwitz. The highest level of German government officials proceeded to kill all Jews in Europe. The property, homes, and jobs were redistributed to German occupiers and non-Jews. Hitler was definitely an example of the dark side of human behavior.

Adolf Hitler was never tried for his crimes because he committed suicide. The Nuremberg trials were held by the Allies against the defeated Nazi German leaders for their atrocities of plotting and carrying out invasions across Europe. Twenty-seven million deaths occurred in the Soviet Union. The defendants were tried for war crimes and crimes against humanity.

Chapter Thirty-Two:
Background of The American Empire

"Those who sacrifice liberty for safety deserve neither."

~Benjamin Franklin

The First Spiritual Awakening that is recorded in the history of the world is credited with helping to inspire a new national identity that served as the impetus for the American Revolution. This marked a new approach to religious worship by a great number of Christian believers. In colonial times, people all over the world began to disassociate themselves from the established approach to the traditional form of worship. Believers in the Judeo-Christian faith became more passionate, with greater fervor and emotion in their expression of worship to God.

Among those who were inspired with greater passion were devotees such as John Wesley, his brother Charles, and George Whitefield in England. These men preached with passion and fired up their followers with vehemence and valor. This passion-filled form of worship crossed over to the American colonies in the first half of the eighteenth century. The religious pilgrims of the American colonies felt a closer connectedness to their Father in heaven. There was an intimate bonding with God that resulted in a spiritual awakening for a great number of new believers.

John Wesley was born in 1703 in Epworth, Lincolnshire, of the United Kingdom. He was the second son of fifteen children born to a preacher of the Anglican Church and a devout mother who led him in prayer and discipline to express his faith. When Wesley came of age, he attended Oxford University. While at Oxford, he joined a group of believers called the "Holy Club."

The members of the "Holy Club" observed strict rules of charity, fasting, and Bible study. Wesley later made the decision to set sail for Georgia in colonial America. As a Protestant missionary, he preached the gospels from the Judeo-Christian Bible. Wesley became disillusioned with his life after a time living in the colonies and decided to return to England.

While attending a Moravian Church meeting in 1758, Wesley experienced a personal spiritual awakening which filled him with vision and direction. He began to hold open church gatherings in fields that offered space for large numbers of people. Wesley reached thousands with his passionate, heartfelt devotions. He traveled more than four thousand miles a year, sharing his devout worship, discipline, and faith.

John Wesley delivered more than 40,000 sermons from the Judeo-Christian Bible. He established schools, clinics, and orphanages. Many of Wesley's sermons contained sayings which became famous quotes. Some of Wesley's quotes are as follows:

1. Do all the good you can, by all the means you can, in all the places you can, to all the people you can, for as long as ever you can.

2. Whosoever will reign with Christ in heaven, must have Christ reigning with him on earth.

3. What one generation tolerates, the next generation will embrace.

John Wesley was an English cleric, theologian, evangelist, and leader of the revival movement within the Church of England of the 1700s, which became known as Methodism. This Protestant denomination still exists today. Wesley believed that the church was not only to convert non-believers but to teach them to become disciples. His fear was that the church members would lose their fire, excitement, and power to be effective disciples of the Lord.

Another great theologian, born in Gloucester, England, who was an evangelist and became a stimulus for revival was George Whitefield. Whitefield was a friend of John Wesley and his brother Charles. Like Wesley, Whitefield also sailed to the colonies in America. His career was spent preaching the evangelistic message from Georgia to Massachusetts and traveling back to England, Scotland, and Wales to do the same.

Others who were ardent participants in promoting this spiritual awakening were Jonathan Edwards, who was a Congregationalist theologian and American revivalist, along with Gilbert Tennent, who became a Presbyterian minister. Tennent was the son of a minister who later established a school for ministers. The Tennent family moved from Ireland to the Pennsylvania colonies in America. Gilbert took a pastorate in New Brunswick, New Jersey.

Evangelical revivals swept Britain and its North American colonies in the 1730s and 1740s. History was permanently affected as Protestant adherents added passion and valor to their religious beliefs. The official motto of the United States is, "In God we trust." The Founding Fathers, who formed the Declaration of Independence, the Bill of Rights, and the U.S. Constitution, wrote those powerful documents based on their faith and trust in the God of creation.

The following is the prayer the President and Father of our Country, George Washington, prayed on June 8, 1783:

> *I now make it my earnest prayer, that God would have the United States in his holy protection, that he would incline the hearts of the citizens to cultivate a spirit of subordination and obedience to government, to entertain a brotherly affection and love for one another, for their fellow citizens of the United States at large, and particularly for the brethren who have served in the field, and finally that he would most graciously be pleased to dispose us all, to do justice, to love mercy, and to demean ourselves with that charity, humility and pacific temper of mind, which were the characteristics of the Divine Author of our blessed Religion, and without an humble imitation of whose example of these things, we can never hope to be a happy Nation.*

> *Amen*

Effort shall be made by Gracegate Ministries International to utilize every form of available media in promoting a spiritual awakening that will reach the most remote corners of the world. Please join me in these ministries as we attempt to voice the need for repentance, profession of faith, and the promise of commitment to God. Now is the time to be bold and speak out. It is also the time to follow in the footsteps of those who have died before us so that we may have the freedom to worship. The statement, "The land of the free because of the brave," should be a motto of inspiration for all of us to be bold and brave!

In these present times, we receive information on morbid facts about murder, the tawdry business of politics, the destructive news about floods, tornadoes, and hurricanes, as well as the sordid reports of our fellowman— such as break-ins, theft, beatings, rape, and murder—which are aired for public scrutiny and judgment. These atrocities are offered during the evening news, and then we are expected to turn the TV off and go peacefully to sleep. Night after night, the same rendition of these conditions incites us to believe that things can be no different. Is there any wonder at the number of anti-anxiety and anti-depressant medications dispensed in our society? Many of us are outraged at the number of atrocities that are increasing in our land.

Some of the people I discuss this topic with place the blame on and express a distrust of the dynamics of politics and the government, as well as the institutions that hold world leadership positions. There are some who put the blame on the "filth" that is shown on television, what is being taught in the schools, or the "disobedient delinquents" with whom our children choose to associate. We are all to blame because we haven't kept our focus on the Lord. We have our own little gods who hold positions of authority and power. Far too often, we bow down before the idols prevalent in our culture—those of power, affluence, and materialism. Again, I quote the Bible:

"If my people who are called by my name, will humble themselves and pray and seek my face and turn from their wicked ways, then I will hear from heaven, and I will heal their land."

(II Chronicles 7:14)

The above scripture tells what we must do to heal our land.

We need a Spiritual Awakening that will reach the most remote corners of the world. Please join me at Gracegate Ministries International as we attempt to voice the need for repentance, profession of faith, and the promise of commitment to God. Now is the time to be bold and speak out. It is also the time to follow in the footsteps of those who have died before us so that we may have freedom to worship.

Since the United States of America is such a young nation, it is easier to follow the history of its growth as well as the political and cultural mores of this nation as compared to the growth of other civilizations. There was great diversity brought to the shores of this new nation from many places on earth. The United States of America has enjoyed a reigning position of enormous power during its young existence.

The colonization of America was influenced by many scientific thinkers such as John Bartram of Pennsylvania, who was a botanist. Bartram was considered to be the greatest botanist in the world during that time. He was commissioned by the British Crown to explore the Allegheny River area to collect plants and seeds, which he shared with scientists in England and Europe. Another scientist during the forming of the American Colonies was David Rittenhouse, a notable astronomer, inventor, clockmaker, surveyor, and public official. He designed many scientific instruments.

Cadwallader Colden was a physician, natural scientist, and lieutenant governor of New York during the formation of the Colonies. Colden came to the colonies from Scotland. Another outstanding genius of the times was Benjamin Rush, a physician who studied at the University of Edinburgh before going to the Colonies. He also signed the Declaration of Independence.

Rush was an educator and the founder of Dickinson College. He was also a delegate to the Continental Congress. Benjamin Franklin was probably one of the more famous of these Founding Father geniuses. Franklin was a statesman, scientist, inventor, and diplomat. He helped draft the Declaration of Independence. Franklin was the only Founding Father to sign all four documents leading to the establishment of the United States of America.

The four documents that gave the thirteen colonies independence were: The Declaration of Independence (1776), The Treaty of Alliance with France (1778), The Treaty of Paris establishing peace with Great Britain (1783), and The U.S. Constitution (1787). This was the era of the philosophical age called "The Age of Enlightenment" of the seventeenth and eighteenth centuries, which had global influences and effects. The Age of Enlightenment was an intellectual and philosophical movement that dominated Europe and had an impact on the Colonial American Colonies. The Founding Fathers of the New England Colonies were pioneers of public education.

They made it possible for the children of America's middle class to receive some form of education. The first schools were operated by the churches. Religion was taught along with reading, writing, and arithmetic. The students sat on hard, wooden benches. The one-room schoolhouses were very plain. They were usually located in the middle of the road because no one wanted to use up good farmland for a school building. The only heat was from the fireplace. Candles were too costly, so the only light came from small windows.

There were few teaching tools. Students wrote with quill pens. Primers were shared in the class. Slates were used to write on since there were no blackboards. Students at all grade levels were taught in the same room by one teacher. Students were not required to attend school but were there by parental choice.

The principal institutions of higher education were Harvard, which was founded in 1636; William and Mary, which was established in the colony of Virginia in 1693; Yale University, established in New Haven, Connecticut, in 1701; and Princeton University, which was formed as a Presbyterian college in 1746 and is located in Princeton, New Jersey. The King's College was created in 1754 by a Royal Charter from King George II as an Anglican college headed by the Church of England.

The King's College, which later became Columbia University, is located in upper Manhattan, New York City. This institution produced some notable revolutionaries such as John Jay and Alexander Hamilton. Queen's College, which was established in 1766, is now Rutgers University. Dartmouth College in Hanover, New Hampshire, was established in 1769.

This group of colleges and universities, along with Brown and Cornell Universities, are referred to as "Ivy League Schools." The Ivy League schools, which offer academic excellence and social elitism, were attended by students from society's upper class. Harvard was the place to train Congregational ministers. Princeton was primarily associated with training Presbyterian ministers.

Religion and education have had a long historical connection. Christian religious groups played an important role in each of the early colonies. Catholics and Protestant believers often did not fraternize with one another. The Protestant Anglican Church had split into traditional Anglicans and

Puritans. The religious atmosphere in Colonial America resembled that of Europe.

It was mandated by law that everyone attended a house of worship, and taxes were levied to pay for ministers and teachers. Congregationalism became an offshoot of the English Puritan movement. During the seventeenth and eighteenth centuries, Christianity gave rise to new movements such as Baptist, Methodist, Quakers, and Unitarians. It was the mindset of most Colonists that they needed legislative protection for their religious freedom.

In the dawn of freedom of the United States of America, the earliest educational textbook used was the Holy Bible. There has been no greater influence in the world than this historical account between mankind and the God of creation. The Bible is revered by Christianity as the Word of God. Most of the scriptural quotes in this book are from the New International Version Study Bible.

Secular humanists and apathetic wayfarers who do not pay homage to God have threatened our safety and existence. Just as the termite can destroy a building from the inside, so can apathy, greed, ungodly leaders, and soldiers of Satan. We have strayed so far from Your Word, Lord. Please hear our cry and heal our land! Please join me in the following prayer:

Dear Heavenly Father,

> *We honor You, glorify You, and Father, we ask Your forgiveness for all the wrongs we have committed. We ask forgiveness for those behaviors that You have taught us that are not acceptable to You and for the things we have not done that we do not recognize because of the scales on our eyes and the hardness of our hearts.*

> *Thank You for promising us that You will be beside us through all the trials and tribulations that come our way. Thank You for sending Your Son to provide salvation and the Holy Spirit to comfort us. Thank You for teaching us how to love. Thank You for promising to heal our land if we abide by Your will!*

> *In Your Son, Jesus' precious name, we pray.*

> *Amen*

Have we gone so far in our apostasy that we frown at spiritual intercession? Hopefully not. For only God can heal our land; it is one of His promises! If God could open the Red Sea so the Israelites could cross and escape punishment from the pursuing Egyptians, He can surely save us from the attacks by the demons of Satan.

We are being sought after by the demons fighting in the army of Satan, the "Father of Lies." He knows how his demise comes about, and he strives to destroy those who oppose him. Satan is the "Prince of the power of the air." He is also the ruler of Hades, which is the Empire of Hell.

Prayer is the most effective weapon that we have at our disposal to combat the craftiness and ploys of the Master of deceit and evil. God is in our presence during our prayers, and Satan does not want to be in God's presence. He will go to great extremes to avoid the presence of God. God grants Satan certain privileges but has him on a short leash.

America has had the blessings of God, the light from God, guidance from God, and overflows with the grace of God. "Our cup runneth over." The following is the prayer of Abraham Lincoln, signed March 30, 1863, from his Proclamation Appointing a National Fast and Prayer Day:

> *We have been the recipients of the choicest bounties of Heaven. We have been preserved these many years, in peace and prosperity. We have grown in numbers, wealth and power, as no other nation has ever grown. But we have forgotten God. We have forgotten the gracious hand which has preserved us in peace, and multiplied and enriched and strengthened us; and we have vainly imagined, in the deceitfulness of our hearts, that all these blessings were produced by some superior wisdom and virtue of our own. Intoxicated with unbroken success, we have become too self-sufficient to feel the necessity of redeeming and preserving grace, too proud to pray to the God that made us!*
>
> *It behooves us to humble ourselves before the offended Power, to confess our national sins, and to pray for clemency and forgiveness. Now, therefore, in compliance with the request, and fully*

concurring in the views of the Senate, I do, by this my proclamation, designate and set apart Thursday, the 30th day of April, 1863, as a day of national humiliation, fasting and prayer. And I do hereby request all the People to abstain on that day, from their ordinary secular pursuits, and to unite at their several places of public worship and their respective homes. In keeping the day holy to the Lord, and devoted to the humble discharge to the religious duties proper to that solemn occasion.

All this being done in sincerity and truth, let us then rest humbly in the hope authorized by the Divine teachings, that the united cry of the Nation will be heard on high, and will be answered with blessings, no less than the pardon of our national sins, and the restoration of our now divided and suffering Country, to its former happy condition of unity and peace.

Amen

It is pointed out by Abraham Lincoln that the people of this nation had become too self-sufficient, too secular, and needed to be reminded who it is that created this nation and graced it with people, resources, abundance of, and accessibility to water. In this present time, need we be reminded that it is our Abba who keeps us healthy and with a sound mind on a daily basis. God knows the number of hairs on our head. It is God who promises to guide us in all our endeavors.

How long will God tolerate the disregard for the way we are to love our fellowman and ourselves? How long will it be before we realize our need for allegiance to Him as Sovereign of heaven and earth? If we study the Bible, we are told that God is a God who loves us, but also that He is a God of wrath. How can we ignore the things considered to be abominations to Him? How disobedient do we have to be before God will take measures to get our attention? Or is that already happening?

The news broadcasts reek of the misfortunes of many, as extremes of weather, heinous crimes, safety measures of the railroads, and other issues become current issues that plague our nation. What will it take to bring us to our knees? How much will God tolerate before He intervenes? Will there be another Sodom and Gomorrah?

The following is the prayer given by President Franklin Delano Roosevelt from the June 6, 1944, D-Day radio broadcast:

> *My Fellow Americans: Last night when I spoke with you about the fall of Rome, I knew at that moment that troops from the United States and our allies were crossing the Channel in another and greater operation. It has come to pass with success thus far. I ask you to join with me in prayer:*

> *Almighty God: Our sons, pride of our Nation, this day have set upon a mighty endeavor, a struggle to preserve our Republic, our religion, and our civilization, and to set free a suffering humanity.*

Lead them straight and true; give strength to their arms, stoutness to their hearts, steadfastness in their faith.

They will need Thy blessings. And for us at home – fathers, mothers, children, wives, sisters and brothers of brave men overseas whose thoughts and prayers are ever with them. Help us Almighty God, to rededicate ourselves in renewed faith in Thee in this hour of great sacrifice.

Many people have urged that I call this Nation into a single day of special prayer. But because the road is long and the desire is great, I ask that our people devote themselves in a continuance of prayer. As we arise to each new day, and again when each day is spent, let words of prayer be on our lips, invoking Thy help to our efforts.

And, O Lord, give us Faith. Give us Faith in Thee; Faith in our sons; Faith in each other; Faith in our united crusade. With Thy blessing, we shall prevail over the unholy forces of our enemy. Help us to conquer the apostles of greed and racial arrogances. Lead us to the saving of our country, and with our sister Nations into a world unity that will surely spell a sure peace. A peace invulnerable to the scheming of unworthy men. And a peace that will let all of men live in freedom, reaping the just rewards of their honest toil.

Thy will be done, Almighty God.

Amen

America experienced a new Awakening, which may be labeled "The Fourth Great Spiritual Awakening." This Spiritual Awakening took place in Wilmore, Kentucky, at Asbury University. On February 8, 2023, students were gathered in Hughes Auditorium to pray for a spiritual renewal. The students experienced such an outpouring of God's Spirit that they lingered in the chapel for days.

Many students expressed a compelling desire to accept the God of Jesus, Mary, and Joseph into their hearts. The revival in Wilmore, Kentucky, lasted for sixteen days. People came from all over the world to witness this Spiritual Awakening. The event in Wilmore, Kentucky, evoked a new interest in religious matters by many.

Chapter Thirty-Three:
America's Sins of Commission

"When a man or a woman wrong another in any way and so is unfaithful to the Lord, that person is guilty and must confess the sin he has committed."

(Numbers 5:6)

What are the sins we commit, often, as "backsliding" believers? There are so many of these transgressions, and these transgressions occur so often that we become hardened to the occurrences. We witness the occurrences so often that we gradually come to view them as "acceptable" thorns in the flesh. And, therein, lies the problem.

We must not allow ourselves to accept any occurrence that is not of God. If it is not acceptable according to the Word of God, turn away as fast as you possibly can from this behavior of evil. When temptation comes knocking at your door, send up a bullet prayer (shoot from the hip). God is overjoyed when we ask for His help to overcome these transgressions.

There are many unacceptable behaviors that cause injustice and disharmony, which lead to harsher problems in our lives. The problem could start with stubbornness, lying, swearing, or perhaps with envy of others. When we begin to believe these "shortcomings" are "just minor little incidences," we find ourselves giving in to lust and perhaps considering having an affair. Possibly, there has been the occurrence of incest that has plagued the family for several generations.

At times, filthy talk flourishes as entertainment. We make excuses for our unacceptable behavior: "Everybody is doing it. I'm not hurting anybody – just having a little fun." It is incredible how one sin paves the way for another, more deplorable act that eventually leads to greater consequences.

Dislike can turn into hate, which can eventually end up in the act of murder. The act of stealing can start with something small and end up with stealing someone's spouse – a sin that uproots a whole family. Divorce is so common in our culture that it is readily acceptable. It is so common in our culture that I wonder why preachers still make the statement in the wedding vows: "Until death do us part?"

Is witchcraft still in existence in our culture? There are certainly occults in existence at present times. The street beside the Country Club where I play tennis is named "Peyton Place." This implies a frequency of "spouse swapping," as was the case in the T.V. series by that name.

I was once approached by a "friend" who asked, "If I would like to get together and participate in a 'swapping of partners' routine?" It didn't take me long to sever activities with that couple. At another time, a male friend brushed the side of my bosom, pretending that it was an "accident." There are times when innocent small talk develops into suggestive conversations that can lead to sexual indulgencies. We should avoid these near occasions of sin.

The problems involving sin can start with entertaining unacceptable ideas in our thoughts. It could possibly be our ego that has been offended. Perhaps our pride has been attacked by someone's unkind remarks. We then possibly seek drugs or alcohol to alter or lessen our painful emotions. Drunkenness is unacceptable to the Lord.

If we don't get relief from emotional pain in some way, we begin to conjure up feelings of resentment and hate. Possibly, we begin to blame our parents for the way we were raised. There are spiritually acceptable responses to address the occurrences of Satan's plots of evil. The biblical suggestion of addressing these atrocities is to hand them over to God and ask for His help in dealing with them.

Be patient and wait on God to offer guidance and a solution to the problems we bring to Him. If we are at fault, He will grant us forgiveness if we ask for it. But all of the aspects of prayer and forgiveness have to be according to His plan. When we follow His plan, our being will overflow with the joy of knowing we are in a right relationship with our Father who loves us.

There will be temporary moments of unhappiness. But even at those times of discomfort, we will experience the joy of knowing that the Lord is caring, forgiving, and faithful at all times. Avoid the near occasion of sin. Do not dwell on sinful behaviors, or there will be consequences.

Apathy, greed, and social injustice are the sins of a society that can bring down an empire. My belief is that the greatest threat to the demise of any single concept, shared belief, or vision of the union of people that make up a nation is the lack of a foundation built and sustained on the Word of God. If this essential element is lacking or tampered with, "there is trouble in Paradise!" There are times that trouble creeps in incident by incident. Other times there is an avalanche of cataclysmic proportions.

When we study the history of the Judeo-Christian world, we discover the rise and fall of the Israelite Nation as the people turned their backs on the Lord God. In our study of the history, geography, cultural, and spiritual events in the early Bible, we begin to understand the dynamics involved in these sacred writings. The significance of these happenings in the Bible takes on a new meaning. We realize that some sinful events were significant for a brief time while others had such significance that they had a negative impact on great empires that will last forever.

Early in biblical history, in the Book of Genesis, Chapter 4, Verse 8, we discover that there was trouble in Paradise – in the Garden of Eden. The son of Adam and Eve slew his brother because of jealousy. Both brothers brought gifts to the Lord, but Abel's gift pleased the Lord more than Cain's. Because this offended Cain, he killed his brother.

In the present times, during the height of the Covid-19 pandemic in 2020, violent crimes rose. Murders rose in 2021. Divorce rates are still higher than they were in the 1970s. Approximately 40–50% of marriages end in divorce. Fewer couples are choosing to marry in our current culture; the trend is to live together without the sacred bonds of marriage.

Baby Boomer divorce rates have increased drastically over the past thirty years. The national divorce rate has almost doubled since 1990. Studies indicate that 28–32 is the best age to get married. Women who obtain a higher education level get divorced less than those with lower levels of education.

When we study the Bible, we read in the book of Exodus, the story of Moses killing an Egyptian soldier.

"He saw an Egyptian beating one of his own people. Glancing this way and that and seeing no one, he killed the Egyptian and hid him in the sand. The next day he went out and saw two Hebrews fighting. He asked the one in the wrong, 'Why are you hitting your fellow Hebrew?' The man said, 'Who made you ruler and judge over us? Are you thinking of killing me as you killed the Egyptian?'"

(Exodus 2:11-14)

The sacrifices and rituals found in Leviticus represent God's covenant with Israel – the Israelites were His people, and He established His rule over all aspects of their lives. God is not always pleased with Israel. In spite of that, He is always faithful to keep His promises. Many Hebrews reside in America. God is faithful to His Chosen people in America, Israel, and worldwide.

The religious faith of most of the Founding Fathers of the American Colonies, which grew into this nation, consisted of orthodox beliefs. Most of the patriots were from one of three religious groups – Anglicanism, which was supported by George Washington (whose name is revered as the "Father" of this country), Congregationalist, and Presbyterian.

George Washington's ancestral family, whose name was Wessington, were from England. His great-great-grandfather attended college in Essex, England. In 1633, he began to serve as pastor of a local church. Although most of Washington's people were from England, his most notable ancestor, the proof provided by history, was Charlemagne, the first ruler of the Holy Roman Empire.

Presbyterianism was the faith claimed by the revolutionaries John Witherspoon and Richard Stockton. James Caldwell was also a Presbyterian minister who played an important part in the American Revolution. Discussions on religious beliefs at that time included the "right to choose the religion of your choice." Caldwell became a chaplain during the American Revolution.

The third religious group was from the Congregationalist faith sector, of which John and Samuel Adams were members. The Founding Fathers' core beliefs were spiritually based. Along with an ethic of hard work, religion provided the guide for moral and ethical values. It was the belief of the Founding Fathers that fighting for freedom was acceptable to God.

Among the Founding Fathers were believers from the Society of Friends (Quakers), Lutherans, and Dutch Reform. There also were three Revolutionaries of the Catholic faith – Charles and Daniel Carroll and Thomas Fitzsimmons. Many were "born again Christians." Most of these Revolutionaries were on Church rolls, had been baptized, and were known to seek Divine assistance. They were married to spouses who were practicing Christians.

In 18th century America, a school of religious thought existed which was referred to as Deism. The Deists agreed with the philosophy of John Locke, Isaac Newton, and Jean-Jacques Rousseau. It was the belief of the Deists that experience and rationality determine the validity of human ideals and behavior rather than church dogma and Scripture. Deism was a topic of discussion in the political circles at that time. Thomas Paine was also a proponent of Deism.

Orthodox Christians among the Founding Fathers include Samuel Adams, John Jay, Elias Boudinot, and Patrick Henry. To accurately make assumptions of one's spiritual beliefs, it was suggested that you read what they have written. Then listen to what they say and watch closely what they do. Read the Bible completely through in order to gain the knowledge of God telling us how to live and love.

Many groups left their homeland to seek freedom of religion in the New World. In 1620, one hundred English Puritans established a small settlement near Plymouth, Massachusetts. These immigrants were mostly from the East Anglican parts of England, which included Norfolk, Suffolk, Essex, as well as Kent and East Sussex. Many settled in Boston and adjacent areas. Large-scale immigration continued until 1700.

Massachusetts, New Hampshire, Connecticut, and Rhode Island were the earliest colonies. They were established along the northeast coastal region. The colonists consisted of skilled farmers, tradesmen, and craftsmen. The first university, Harvard, was established to train ministers needed for the colonies.

The number of colonists grew rapidly until, by 1790, there were approximately 900,000 people inhabiting this region. Dutch immigrants arrived and established the city of New Amsterdam, which was later named New York. Pennsylvania was settled by the Quakers. There was a strong German infiltration located in the villages along the Delaware River valley.

Chapter Thirty-Four:
America's Sins of Omission

"Anyone, then who knows the good he ought to do and does not do it, sins."

(James 4:17)

Early settlers in America were the trespassers who literally forced the American Indians from the land they had hunted on, built tepees for warmth and safety from animals, weather, and other warring tribes. These trespassers were guilty of sins of commission. They were also guilty of sins of omission. How many thousands of lives on both sides were lost?

The Native Americans were called savages by the interlopers. Was this name-calling justification for the slaughter and genocide of a race, a civilization—an empire? Nothing—no explanation—can justify the extinction of any of God's children. I do not want to be guilty of judging past happenings from the advantage of weighing the events, consequences, and results gleaned from the perspective of looking back.

Another concurring set of wrongdoings that has been ongoing since the beginning of time are the atrocities committed by mankind in the form of abuse of the animals and the land that was given to man by their Creator for their temporary use. I can't describe these atrocities nearly as well as the Christian, libertarian, environmentalist, capitalist, and farmer-author Joel Salatin. My hero, Joel Salatin, states:

"The point is that the sum and substance of our lives should point toward the goodness of God. And he wants us to understand that how we extend that respect and honor to His creation indicates our level of honoring His specialness . . . if we can't appreciate the pigness of the pig, we can't appreciate the Godness of God."

Salatin references the Bible throughout his writings. He supports his views with Scripture. Joel Salatin is both brave and bold. This pig farmer fights for what he believes is God's plan for how we are to treat what He graciously gave us dominion over, with all the responsibilities that accompany His plan.

This brave farmer, who named his farm "Polyface, Inc.," which means "Farm of Many Faces," has struggled with bureaucracies and rigid legislature that makes things that seem to be common sense into activities that break the law. An example of this is as follows: "I want to dress my beef and pork on the farm where I've coddled and raised it. But zoning laws prohibit slaughterhouses on agricultural land. The government has so many restrictions on this activity: I am breaking the law if I sell meat for food that has been slaughtered on my land."

Bureaucratic restrictions are so diabolical, they allow injecting hormones into animals to increase profits, which have detrimental effects. Humans ingest the hormone-laden animals. Could this possibly lead to the rise of cancer and other debilitating outcomes in our culture? Is this what God intended when He gave us dominion over animals?

Another sin that has reached an all-time high in today's world is abortion. Six out of ten of all unintended pregnancies end in abortion. Why isn't adoption offered instead of abortion? Abortion clinics have recently been referred to as the settings for the "new holocaust." Mothers are given legal permission to murder their babies. Helpless embryos are cut to pieces or destroyed by chemical means.

Is this what God intended to happen to the future heirs of His Kingdom? Why are we allowing these abhorrent acts to continue? We are just as accountable for those things we do not do as for the transgressions we commit. If we reflect on thoughts along these lines and do some mental calisthenics, we will begin to see the truth of this idea. We may possibly come to realize that the idea of "sins of omission" has merit. What we don't do can have great consequences.

So, what have I been neglecting to act upon? Thoughts come to mind of some areas that I have not been as active in as I possibly could have been. At times, I fail to get my negligent self out to the polls to vote. We have a responsibility to be active in the political arena. There are some caring politicians who need our votes. They have proven themselves worthy in the public domain.

In introspection, I must admit there are instances when I fail to be bold and speak my mind when I am aware that an injustice has been committed. Do

I always return excess money when an overamount is given back to me in error? Am I as aware as I should be about the need to proselytize for new members or converts to Christianity? How many times have I failed to give empathy or support to someone when they are going through difficult times?

The commandment to love our neighbor is a debt we can never pay in full. The laws given to Moses by God gave us moral laws. Scripture offers advice, suggestions, and warnings in the stories provided to us. Romans 6:14 states:

"For sin shall not be your master, because you are not under the law, but under grace."

In this Epistle, Paul was talking to the people of the church in Rome, who probably were mostly Gentiles with a minority of Jews. Paul was possibly in Corinth when he wrote or dictated this epistle to a scribe. He wrote about God's plan of salvation and righteousness for the Jew and Gentile alike. Although the theme addresses the righteousness of God, it also brings up issues of guilt and sanctification.

The majority, a Gentile group in the church, were rejecting the Jews who still felt it necessary to observe feast days and dietary restrictions as being sacred. Since Paul had received contributions from missionary churches he had already visited, he felt it necessary to return to Jerusalem with the offerings. So, Paul wrote to the church in Rome to prepare the way for a future visit.

Paul had great concern for the salvation of Israel. He contrasted man's unrighteousness with God's gift of righteousness (Christ). Paul sets forth the means by which God instills righteousness in man. He brought up man's victory over sin through the redemptive work of Christ on the cross.

Chapter Thirty-Five:
The Sinister Sixties – A Decade of Revolution - Part I

"Everyone must commit himself to the governing author-ties, for there is no authority except that which God has established . . . he who rebels against authority is against what God has instituted . . ."

(Romans 13:1-2)

The Sixties have gone down in history as being known for the number of counter-culture movements that erupted in that decade. It was a time when ordinary citizens questioned the ideals of the nation's democratic policies. The Sixties were a decade of revolution. The people began to question the very things they had previously thought they held close to their hearts.

The Sinister Sixties ushered in a time when America flagrantly began to turn away from God. The people's faith in God was tested. The President's religious affiliations were questioned. Homosexuality, proclaimed an abomination to God, became a "politically acceptable" behavior.

The word "gay" took on a new meaning. It no longer meant acting "carefree" or being "bright and exceptionally happy people." It was socially unacceptable to speak critically of "Gay" people. Men who acted effeminate were stereotyped as being "Gay." Females who showed typical male characteristics were called "Butch." Movies began showing scenes of male-male and female-female relationships on the screen.

Laws began to be challenged in court because hospitals would not let a "Gay partner" in to visit his or her sick "partner." Previously, being questioned if a Gay couple would make capable parents was challenged. "Should Gay partners be allowed the same insurance benefits as in a heterosexual relationship?" was questioned as fair or not.

The "dawn of the Golden Age" began in 1961, as handsome and charismatic John Fitzgerald Kennedy was inaugurated as president of the United States of America on January 20. He was from Boston's most prominent Catholic family. He had served in the U.S. Navy. He also served in both the House of Representatives and the Senate.

President Kennedy had promised an ambitious platform during his campaign. His relationship with the business community had been damaged when Roger Blough, president of U.S. Steel Corporation, decided to increase the price of steel. At that time, Kennedy was a member of the U.S. Senate.

JFK was against Blough's increase in the price of steel. This caused many to distrust the senator's support of business interests. Kennedy's slogan as a candidate for president was, "The government possesses big answers to big problems." JFK campaigned on the promise of a "New Frontier." The proposed price increase of steel was canceled.

While serving in Congress, Kennedy had attacked French colonization in Vietnam, Algeria, and sub-Saharan Africa. This was in direct conflict with the Soviet Union's political aspirations. The leaders of the two superpowers—the USA and the Soviet Union—began political maneuvers: arms build-up programs, economic aid to third world nations, and proxy wars between nations. The two superpowers, that had been Allies during WWII, became adversaries in a "Cold War."

The Warsaw Pact, created in 1955, was referred to as "The Eastern Bloc." This was an alliance between Eastern countries that helped to strengthen their political powers. The Soviet Union set up pro-communist regimes in Poland, Hungary, Bulgaria, Czechoslovakia, Romania, Albania, and East Germany. The United States responded with a containment policy to prevent the spread of communism in Western European nations.

The USA also redirected the policy of not getting involved in European politics. Shortly after WWII, the powers to be in the U.S. started a series of policies to prevent communist subversive activities. The Truman Doctrine of 1947 promised aid to governments threatened by communist subversion. The efforts of George Marshall culminated in The Marshall Plan, which provided billions of dollars of economic assistance to countries to eliminate political instabilities that could pave the way for communist takeovers.

The United States joined NATO—the North Atlantic Treaty Organization. This organization attempted to act as a mediator to encourage dialogue between the conflicting superpowers. President Kennedy wanted "to get America going again" by promoting progressive social programs. He began by attacking unemployment problems.

But the issue that became the priority in the early Sixties was the war between North and South Vietnam. In the early days of the presidency, Kennedy was faced with both opportunity and challenge. Fidel Castro's conquest in the overthrow of Fulgencio Batista in Cuba, his inflammatory anti-American remarks, and attacks on U.S. companies instilled an atmosphere of distrust of Fidel Castro in the minds of Americans. Added to this distrust was Castro's close relationship with the Soviet Union.

Before JFK took office, Eisenhower ordered the C.I.A. to train and arm a group of Cuban exiles to return to Cuba to stir up dissension. Ike hoped this would result in an insurrection against Castro. Kennedy inherited this program when he became president. Fidel Castro's communist-supported efforts had overthrown Fulgencio Batista's rule of Cuba.

The U.S. had supported Batista. The Cuban dictator and former soldier was defeated by Castro with the help of Che Guevara, a South American revolutionary. America continued to oppose Castro and his leftist ideologies. Upper-class professionals, doctors, businessmen, and their families began leaving Cuba to seek refuge in the U.S.

On April 20, 1961, fourteen hundred Cuban exiles, covertly supported, directed, and financed by the United States of America, landed on the southwestern coast of Cuba at the Bay of Pigs. This peaceful cove is slightly more than a hundred miles from Havana, the capital of Cuba. Their intent was to create an uprising to overthrow the power of Castro's revolution. The invasion was unsuccessful.

In October of 1962, photographs of nuclear missile sites being built by the Soviet Union in Cuba were taken by an American U-2 plane. President Kennedy and his advisors met in secret for several days. They proceeded to study the issues around this threatening discovery. Does this mean the beginning of WWIII?

President Kennedy's decision was to place a ring of ships around the island to prevent Soviets from bringing in supplies to Cuba. No one could predict how Nikita Khrushchev would retaliate to the U.S. blockade and the demands made by JFK. The atmosphere of the nuclear threat was a worldwide concern. Both superpowers recognized the possibility of a war that could bring on the end of times.

The severity of the nuclear threat brought about the removal of the missiles from Cuba by the Soviets. William Burr and Leopoldo Nuti examined Kennedy's administration's efforts to remove missiles that were a threat to other nations. Kennedy agreed to remove U.S. Jupiter missiles from Turkey and Italy. This was all done in secrecy with Nikita Khrushchev and resulted in the end of the Cuban Missile Crisis. The possibility of nuclear war, at that moment in time, was defused.

When reviewing world history, we discover there were political differences between the superpowers following World War II. The Allied Powers, at the end of the War, divided Germany into two zones. The two zones consisted of East Germany and West Germany. The Soviet Union was given control of East Germany. West Germany's occupation was shared by the WWII Allies: Great Britain, France, and the United States.

The differences between the Soviet's Communist ideology and that of the Western alliances created a rivalry between the countries. This rivalry was first described by English writer George Orwell as being a "Cold War." Orwell's article described a "nuclear stalemate" between the two superpowers. The term was first used in a speech in the House of Representatives in Columbia, South Carolina, by Bernard Baruch. He was there for the unveiling of his portrait.

Baruch was a millionaire who had served as an advisor at the Paris Peace Talks that ended WWI. Baruch had advised, under Woodrow Wilson, Franklin D. Roosevelt, and Harry S. Truman. His field of expertise was in economic and foreign policy. Baruch was famous for his speech declaring that, "Only through unity between labor and management, could the United States hope to play its role as the major force by which the world could renew itself physically and spiritually."

The Soviets had installed left-wing governments in the countries they had liberated during WWII by their Red Army. Fearing another threat from Germany, the Soviets were determined to maintain control of Eastern Europe. They sought to spread communism throughout the world. They based their political beliefs on the dogma of Karl Marx.

Marx believed in "the establishment of a communist society centered on common ownership of the means of production with free access to the articles of consumption." This view was an attempt to end the exploitation of labor. I do not claim to be an expert on socio-economics or communism, but I have enjoyed four trips to Russia and have shopped in the communist department store, Gum (pronounced Goom), located in Red Square in Moscow. I discovered that a hierarchy of Communist autocrats have first choice to obtain the goods offered in the store.

Being eligible to obtain products seems to depend on one's level in the party. That concept does not seem fair to me. The same restrictions are observed when acquiring housing, vacations, or automobiles. The quality of life is very much dependent on who you are and what rank you hold in the party.

As we continue studying the history of WWII, we discover the Allies of West Germany agreed to rebuild the country as a capitalist democracy. Although Berlin was two hundred miles inside East Germany, it was divided into two zones – East Berlin and West Berlin. Construction to build a wall to separate East and West Germany began on August 13, 1961. This wall was called "The Iron Curtain."

Dissatisfaction with the conditions that existed in East Germany led to great numbers of people crossing the wall into West Germany. Armed guards were placed along the wall to keep people from going from East to West Germany. More than one hundred people died from trying to cross the corridor between the East and West, known as the "death strip." There was no military combat during the Cold War; there was only propaganda, proxy wars, and political maneuvers.

When we continue to review the happenings of the 1960s decade, we learn that Vietnam was part of French colonial rule in Indochina. In the early days of the presidency, Kennedy, along with his advisors, believed that America's policy concerning involvement in the war in Vietnam presented a means to thwart efforts of unstable countries to form newly independent communist nations in Asia and Africa.

This meant American policy regarding Vietnam would model the means to overthrow shaky new governments leaning toward communism in emerging nations. President Kennedy considered Vietnam a cornerstone of the free world. The Viet Cong had assassinated 2,500 government-related people since the beginning of their insurgence. Kennedy decided to uphold the commitments made to Vietnam by the Truman and Eisenhower administrations. He would not get involved in Vietnam without carefully analyzing and getting input from his advisors.

It was the theory of those advising Kennedy that losing the war in Vietnam would affect the welfare of other independent nations. This effect was known as "The Domino Theory." This theory postulated that when one nation fell, others would also fall as dominoes do when pushed while standing on end in a long line. Each domino knocks down the next domino in line, creating a rippling wave until the last domino falls.

Troops were deployed to Vietnam to train, advise, and support the South Vietnamese. By the summer of 1963, more than one hundred Americans had been killed or were missing in action. The war was continuing to go badly for those who fought Ho Minh Chou. Many American citizens thought that the U.S. should not be involved in the Vietnam War.

On November 23, 1963, while riding in a presidential motorcade traveling in Dallas, Texas' Dealey Park, JFK was shot. The bullets proved to be fatal. Kennedy had been assassinated. His wife, Jacqueline; Texas governor John Connally; and his wife, Nellie, were also in the same vehicle. A former Marine, Lee Harvey Oswald, who had briefly lived in Russia, was thought to be behind the assassination. Oswald was later shot and killed by Jack Ruby, a nightclub owner.

In October 1967, 70,000 protestors participated in a massive Vietnam War protest at the nation's capital in Washington, D.C. The view of the protestors was that the U.S. was supporting a corrupt dictatorship in Saigon. The protest began with a gathering around the Lincoln Memorial. After a time, 50,000 of the protestors marched across the Potomac to the Pentagon, where they were confronted by soldiers. There is a famous photograph of a protestor placing flowers around the end of a rifle.

On January 31, 1968, a 70,000-men military force under the Democratic Vietnam Republic (DVR) launched a series of attacks on one hundred villages and cities in South Vietnam. After Kennedy's assassination, Vice President Lyndon Johnson had been sworn in as president. He made a speech in March of 1968, which met with a positive response, and peace talks between North Vietnam and the U.S. began. Richard M. Nixon, following Johnson's presidency, directed the U.S. forces to secretly bomb North Vietnamese base camps in Cambodia and Laos. This escalation in bombing brought no positive results in peace negotiations.

Henry Kissinger, an American diplomat, played a prominent role in the governmental policies concerning the Vietnam War. He was the delegate representing the U.S. at peace conferences. In 1968, Kissinger leaked information from one of the conferences to Nixon. When elected president, Richard Nixon appointed Kissinger as National Security Adviser. Henry Kissinger made efforts to end the war in Vietnam on American terms.

In the United States, a group of National Guards opened fire on students at Kent State University in Ohio on May 4, 1970. These students were protesting the war. Four students were killed, and several were wounded. Protests caught on at other college campuses. Studies indicate that 58% of the people thought the war in "Nam" to be immoral.

On January 27, 1973, the Paris Peace Accords were signed, and Vietnam was unified under the name of "The Socialist Republic of Vietnam." Fighting continued after this; the population in Vietnam was drastically diminished. Returning soldiers to the U.S. were treated with scorn, frowned on, and sometimes spit upon. The wounded, the wheelchair-bound, and many suffering from Agent Orange poisoning held their own parade down Pennsylvania Avenue in front of the White House.

Chapter Thirty-Six:
The Sinister Sixties – A Decade of Revolution - Part II

"Remind them to be submissive to rulers and authorities, to be obedient, to be ready for every good work . . ."

(Titus 3:1)

The fight for racial equality in the U.S. had been a continuing struggle since Blacks had been brought to America. Racial unrest demanded to be dealt with once again. Repudiation of the Jim Crow laws encouraged challenges between ethnic factions and became a political issue in the sixties. Jim Crow was the term used for an African-American.

The Southern states had their own state laws concerning the segregation of Blacks and Whites. Basically, the two ethnic groups were to have separate accommodations such as education, housing, transportation, eating, and restrooms. This separation also extended to the availability of medical care, retail stores, and beauty and barber shops. Virtually, the everyday existence of the two ethnic groups was to be separated in the Southern states.

The Sixties were a period of anger and protests between the Blacks and Whites. Bold individuals emerged that dared to demand equality between the races. One of those individuals was Reverend Dr. Martin Luther King

Jr., a Black minister of the Baptist faith. He became one of the most notable activists in the Civil Rights Movement from 1955 to his assassination in 1968.

King raised public awareness of the injustices of segregation. He became involved in local grassroots campaigns protesting the injustices of racial discrimination. The first such incident was when an African-American woman named Rosa Parks, in Montgomery, Alabama, refused to give her seat up to a white male. She was arrested for her struggle to demand justice. King chose to use tactics such as this to emphasize the injustices of discrimination. He directed an effective retaliation to Rosa Parks' arrest.

Under the direction of Reverend King, the African-American community boycotted the public transportation system of Montgomery, Alabama. After a year of such action, the United States Supreme Court ruled in Browder v. Gayle that bus segregation was unconstitutional. During the months following this incident, King emphasized the banning of racial segregation on all public buses. He dared to push for justice by initiating non-violent sit-ins and protest marches.

While in a Birmingham, Alabama, jail, King wrote an eloquent letter claiming the need for multiple forces to conduct efforts such as peaceful protestation. He believed that radical action was needed to dramatize the need for change. King was a follower of the power of India's Mahatma Gandhi's peaceful protesting. Reverend Martin Luther King proved his point and raised the awareness level of segregation injustices.

The struggle for civil rights continued to be a defining factor in the sinister Sixties. Such acts as four Black students sitting down at a Whites-only lunch counter in Greensboro, North Carolina, demanding to be served lunch gave proof of the demand for justice. Following this event, tens of thousands of people, demanding the right to be served at "White-only lunch counters" across the world, sat down in protest of moral injustice. Martin Luther King believed in the scripture from the Bible found in Galatians 3:28:

"There is neither Jew nor Greek, slave nor free, male nor female, for you are all one in Christ, Jesus."

MLK led a peaceful Civil Rights march from Selma to Montgomery, Alabama. He delivered speeches which included famous quotes such as:

"Injustice anywhere is a threat to justice everywhere. The time is always right to do what is right. Darkness cannot drive out darkness, only light can do that. Hate cannot drive out hate, only love can do that. I have a dream, that one day this nation will rise up and live out the true meaning of its creed, We hold these truths to be self-evident, that all men are created equal."

The impact of King's non-violent protests swayed opinions and became the impetus for the creation of the Civil Rights Act of 1964. This act gave the federal government the right to enforce desegregation of public places and outlawed discrimination in all publicly owned facilities. King's popularity soared. He was notified that he was to be a recipient of the Nobel Peace Prize.

During the acceptance speech, MLK stated: "I refuse to accept the idea that the 'ishness' of man's present nature makes him morally incapable of reaching up for the eternal 'oughtness' that forever confronts him." There was scandalous talk about King being involved in extra-marital affairs. Could this have been a "thorn in the flesh" as described by Paul, the thirteenth apostle?

I choose to not judge King by any standard other than scripture:

"Every good tree bears good fruit, but a bad tree bears bad fruit. A good tree cannot bear bad fruit, and a bad tree cannot bear good fruit."

(Matthew 7:17)

MLK often became discouraged and wrote the following in 1963: "Living every day under the threat of death, I feel discouraged every now and then and feel that my work is in vain, but then the Holy Spirit revives my soul again." On April 3, 1968, the night before he died, King told a crowd at the Mason Temple Church in Memphis, "I've seen the Promised Land. I may not get there with you, but I want you to know tonight that we, as a people, will get to the Promised Land."

King traveled to Memphis to assist sanitation workers during a strike. The next day, as he stood on the balcony of the Lorraine Motel, Reverend

Doctor Martin Luther King was shot down by a sniper's bullet. The name of the killer remains a controversy. James Earl Ray confessed to the crime and was imprisoned for the act.

Ray later recanted and stated that he was not responsible for King's death. King's family does not believe that he was responsible for the death of their loved one. As with the assassination of John Fitzgerald Kennedy, will we ever know the facts and the truth surrounding these deplorable killings?

Two major books on Dr. King's contributions to the Civil Rights Movement, David J. Garrow's *Bearing the Cross* (1986) and Taylor Branch's *Parting the Waters* (1988), were awarded Pulitzer Prizes. MLK was deeply committed to attaining social justice through peaceful means. Legislation to establish a Martin Luther King federal holiday was signed by President Ronald Reagan on November 3, 1983. King's legacy emphasizes a commitment to democratic and Christian ideals.

There were younger, more militant Blacks who thought King's protests and sit-ins were "criminal." Malcolm X, one of Martin Luther King's critics, had this to say concerning nonviolence: "It is criminal to teach a man not to defend himself when he is the constant victim of brutal attacks." MLK and Malcolm X differed in their faith and ideology. Both were leading Civil Rights activists. Both men had a following of supporters eager to carry out the message proclaimed by their leader.

Martin Luther King Jr. was a Baptist minister who believed in the Judeo-Christian faith. He had a "dream" in which he saw a world where his children would be judged by the merits of their character, not the color of their skin. MLK once met racial injustice activist Malcolm X. They were oppositional in their methods of protest, but shared the hope of raising awareness of the injustices of racial discrimination and abolishing racial prejudices.

When he was born, Malcolm was given the surname of his father—Little. He later took the famous "X" to represent the name of his unknown African ancestral surname before the slave traders brought his ancestors to America. He was born, the fourth of seven children, on May 19, 1925, in Omaha, Nebraska. His father was a Baptist lay leader and follower of Marcus Garvey. Garvey started the first important American Black activist movement in Harlem, New York.

Malcolm X was born into a poor family who were harassed by the Ku Klux Klan. When Malcolm was six years old, his father died. Shortly after that, his mother, Louise, was hospitalized for mental instabilities. He lived with relatives and foster families.

He spent time in jail as a youth for petty theft. When he was in his early twenties, he was arrested for burglary and sent to prison. While in prison, Malcolm received a book from his brother about Islam and the Muslim beliefs. He met other Black Muslim prisoners in jail and became involved in their discussions on the beliefs of the Islamic faith.

When he got out of prison, he joined the Nation of Islam and became a public representative for twelve years. In later speeches, Malcolm expressed pride in the Islamic Nation's social welfare programs such as drug rehabilitation. Malcolm X traveled around the world giving talks on social injustices of people of color. He aroused resentment toward injustice in the Black communities.

There are five basic tenets in the Islamic faith, which are called the Pillars of Islam. These are the fundamental beliefs that are considered to be obligatory acts of worship for all Muslims. The pillars of faith can be found in the Hadith of Gabriel. The five pillars are centered around: (1) The Muslim Creed, (2) Prayer, (3) Charity to the poor, (4) Fasting in the month of Ramadan, and (5) Making a pilgrimage to Mecca once a year.

Malcolm X later became disillusioned with the Nation of Islam and its leader, Elijah Muhammad. In the Islamic belief, Muslim believers are expected to make a pilgrimage to Mecca in Saudi Arabia every year. Mecca is the place where Mohammed, the Prophet, supposedly ascended into heaven. This pilgrimage is called a Hajj.

Malcolm X was a Muslim who thought Blacks and Whites should live separately and, because of their differences, could never be integrated. Malcolm X changed his views on the Muslim faith but never accepted MLK's faith or ideology. He was a prominent Civil Rights leader. Malcolm Little, known as Malcolm X, was assassinated in 1965.

Change was the buzzword during the Sixties. Changes in fashion included going from straight-legged trousers to bell bottoms. The miniskirt was introduced in London and caused an instant fashion craze. The most popular vehicles were Lee Iacocca's Ford Mustang, the Shelby Cobra, and the Volkswagen Beetle.

Pop culture gave rise to the Lava Lamp, the Peace Symbol, and "free love." The Spider-Man comic character appeared in the *Amazing Fantasy* comic book. The "flower power" generation listened to the Beatles, the Mods, and the Who musical groups. The audio cassette was invented. The video cassette recorder became the "in-thing" to own.

Owning a television set became a new norm. The longest-running "soap opera" started at the beginning of the Sixties. Live broadcasts began on the scene. British Broadcasting Corporation (BBC) went on the air in 1964. It was the first network to offer color TV.

Sam Walton opened the first Walmart store in Arkansas. This was a change from the "Mom and Pop" retail stores of the past. The USA began to use ZIP codes in the address system. Sidney Poitier was the first Black to win an Academy Award from the motion picture industry in Hollywood.

Songwriter-singer Robert Allen Zimmerman changed his name to Bob Dylan, partly because he was inspired by the poet Dylan Thomas, but mostly because he liked the way it sounded. Dylan made a name for himself in a coffeehouse in New York's Greenwich Village. He had a natural fondness for folk music and an inherent dislike of war. He wrote the following lyrics to the song he called *The Times They Are a-Changin'*:

The times they are a-changing

come, gather 'round, people

wherever you roam

and admit that the waters

around you have grown.

and accept it that soon

you'll be drenched to the bone.

if your time to you is worth savin'

you better start swimmin'

or you'll sink like a stone.

for the times they are a-changin'

On the more serious side, many world happenings occurred, such as African nations succeeding from European control. Cote D'Ivoire, Chad, Benin, the Islamic country of Mauritania, Senegal, and the Central African Republic received their independence from France in the 1960s. The Organization of Petroleum Exporting Countries (OPEC) was formed.

Yuri Gagarin, a Soviet cosmonaut, became the first man in space. Alan Shepard became the first American in space. NASA's Mariner 4 spaceship approached Mars and offered photographs of outer space for the first time. The Beginner's All-purpose Symbolic Instruction Code (B.A.S.I.C.) was introduced to the world in 1963.

At the Ambassador Hotel on July 6, 1968, Sirhan Sirhan fired the fatal shot that killed Robert Francis Kennedy, the brother of assassinated President John Kennedy. Like his brother John, RFK served as senator before being appointed U.S. Attorney General when his brother became president. The parents of JFK and Robert Kennedy were Joseph P. Kennedy and Rose Fitzgerald Kennedy. Joe and Rose Kennedy had nine children.

JFK and Robert were survived by another brother, Edward (Ted), who also served as a senator and served more than forty-six years in the U.S. Senate. How many political leaders of times past were victims of assassination? Who would murder Christian freedom-fighters? What can we do as Christians to prevent these atrocities from happening?

The answer lies in the struggle to exemplify the Word of God for which King dedicated his life. Martin Luther King lived under the threat of harassment, incarceration, and assassination. But he chose to continue his struggle because he was a man of faith with a vision from God. The Sixties brought about big changes and smaller ones.

It was during that decade of change that electric trains became popular as the means of inner-city transportation. Another significant change during that decade was the United Kingdom abolishing the death penalty. Thurgood Marshall was the first African American to be appointed to the Supreme Court. Indira Gandhi became the first woman to become Prime Minister of India.

The first Super Bowl hosted the Green Bay Packers against the Kansas City Chiefs. The Packers won with a score of 35 to 10. Technology was enhanced by the computer mouse, video conferencing, teleconferencing, and e-mail. ARPANET—the Advanced Research Projects Agency Network, a research-oriented prototype for academic and research projects—was introduced in 1969.

Neil Armstrong and Buzz Aldrin, on the Apollo 11 mission, became the first men on the moon. On June 21, 1969, the police were called out to respond to a disturbance at the "Gay" bar in the Stonewall Inn, located in Greenwich Village, which is a neighborhood in lower Manhattan in New York City. This incident proved to have lasting consequences. The Gay patrons were tired of what they felt was harassment and discrimination. They overcame the police, locking the patrons inside the bar and holding them hostage.

Fire erupted, neighbors joined in the protests and demonstrations, and supporters joined the riot that lasted for two nights. On the anniversary of the Stonewall Inn event held the following year, Gay pride marches were held in Chicago, Los Angeles, New York, and San Francisco. Gay rights organizations, such as the LGBT, were established across America and around the world. Events are held each year during June in honor of the Stonewall Uprising and to celebrate "Gay Pride."

Three newspapers were established to promote the right for Gays to live openly regarding their sexual orientation. This presents a conundrum for believers in the Christian faith. Since Sodom and Gomorrah were destroyed because of their homosexual activities, by a rain of sulphur, how will God deal with the current Gay involvement? In Romans 1:27, the apostle Paul states explicitly:

"In the same way men also abandoned natural relations with women and were inflamed with lust for one another. Men committed indecent acts with other men, and received unto themselves the due penalty for their perversion."

In the summer of 1969, on Max Yasgur's dairy farm near the city of Bethel, just forty miles southwest of Woodstock, New York, more than 400,000 people gathered to celebrate the largest music festival ever attended. It was being advertised as an "Aquarian Exposition – The Music and Art Festival." It was more commonly referred to as Woodstock Rock Festival for the "peace and love generation." "Straight" people often referred to the event as "a gathering of hippies at an outdoor rock festival."

Many men grew a beard and wore their hair long. Women appeared who, purposely, did not shave their legs or armpits. The "V" sign was commonly waved as an expression for victory. The peace symbol, made up of semaphore flag signals with initials "N" and "D" meaning "Nuclear Disarmament," was painted or sewn on T-shirts or bell-bottom jeans.

There were groupings of free sexual encounters. Plenty of marijuana or "weed" was passed around, as was common during rock concerts. Artie Kornfeld, a promoter, approached Warner Brothers to solicit finances for the festival. After much persuasion, $100,000 was obtained to finance the entire gig.

A stage was built out in a pasture by a pond. A music system was set up. Toilet facilities were installed. Tents were erected. Thirty-two rock acts were presented to the attendees for their pleasure.

What wasn't under the control of the promoters and facilitators was the weather. Rain began to drizzle. Everything, including people, got soaked. The stage and many accommodations were located in a low spot draining down to the pond. Some attendees went skinny-dipping in the pond.

An attempt to sell tickets had been made, but no one planned for the hundreds of people who just showed up and expected accommodations. It turned out to be a miserable mud pit because of three days of sporadic rains. Many of the most popular rock and roll musical groups of the times were featured. Janis Joplin, Jimi Hendrix, The Grateful Dead, The Who, and The Family Stone were among the headliners scheduled to appear. They were airlifted in and out of the gathering at a nearby airfield.

It was reported that there were eight hundred and forty-six "foot lacerations" that needed minor medical attention. There were at least two births and several miscarriages. Providing proper food, water, and sanitation became problematic on the 600-acre farm. Reporter Ethel Romm of the Middleton Times Herald Record called the accommodations "ghetto conditions."

Doctor William Abruzzi was designated as the physician hired to oversee the medical needs of the attendees. The number of medical issues required that doctors and nurses be flown in from neighboring towns. One of the medical problems involved the issue of people who experienced "bad trips" from recreational drugs. According to records furnished by Dr. Abruzzi, seven hundred and forty-two overdoses were reported throughout the festival. Of this number of overdoses, twenty-eight required medical attention.

There were two deaths during the musical festival. Raymond Mizsak, a seventeen-year-old male, was run over by a tractor while he slept in his sleeping bag. The second person to die was an eighteen-year-old Marine, Richard Bieler, who was to be deployed to Vietnam. He reportedly died of a drug overdose. Despite the conditions, the medical problems, the deaths, scarcity of food, and poor sanitation, the majority of the attendees survived. History was made – good and bad.

Although the Sixties brought empowerment to some, it also created polarization of the people as well as the government. The protesting and sinister Sixties went down as an uprising of countercultures.

Chapter Thirty-Seven:
The Enron Energy Fraud

"We are the good guys. We are on the side of the angels."

~Jeffrey Skilling, C.E.O. of Enron

One of the best examples that represents the dark side of human behavior is that of Enron Energy Corporation leaders. Enron was founded in 1985. This energy entity emerged from the action of joining Houston Natural Gas with InterNorth Corporation, which had been operating since the 1930s. The person responsible for this new corporation was Kenneth Lay – the son of a minister.

Enron Corporation became an energy-providing company based in Houston, Texas. It was considered by brokerage houses to be the most outstanding investment venture of the times. The initial activities of this corporation appeared to be like those of any energy company. As time passed, fraudulent activities by Enron's leaders began – the books were being misrepresented, and fraudulent companies were being listed in the files, even though they were non-existent.

Kenneth Skilling, who previously worked for McKenzie Accounting Firm, was hired in 1987 as Enron's C.E.O. Jeffrey Fastow was hired in 1990. Fastow was hired because of his business acumen. He was known for the ability to put a company on the fast track to success. These leaders played a significant role in the rise and fall of Enron.

In retrospect, the clandestine, undercover activities probably began a short time after hiring these two powerful men. Enron leadership, consisting of Chief Executive Officers, Chief Financial Officers, division heads, department heads, and others, were taking part in the devious operations. This fraudulent conspiracy consisted of misappropriating billions of dollars and channeling it into their private bank accounts. Later, when questioned, those involved in this injustice put on a façade of innocence that would impress the members of the Academy Award Nominating Committee for Best Actor in Hollywood. They had one hand on your arm and the other hand in your wallet.

Companies, which in reality did not exist, were listed on records. Activities which did not happen were fabricated, recorded, and placed in the files. Several rooms of falsified records existed. Memos containing information on non-existent energy plants were sent to various employees. This behavior was devious, fraudulent, unlawful, and immoral.

The 20,600 employees of Enron were advised to invest their pension plan (401-k) monies contributed by the employees in Enron stock. The C.E.O.s and C.F.O.s created a "new philosophy" for the process of corporate operations – "Steal as much money from the company as can be generated and deposit the money in your personal bank account."

Billions of dollars in profits were reported as losses. Skilling and Fastow went rogue. Jeffrey Skilling had always had a "wiseass" personality. He was asked during an interview for entrance into Harvard's MBA program, "Do you think you are smart?" His reply was, "I am f - - king smart."

Skilling projected a macho personality. This macho behavior was supported by the fact that he was a rogue motorcyclist – taking risks by participating in challenging and somewhat dangerous events for cyclists. He made friends in the right places. He was the political liaison for Enron.

Enron leaders found ways to "cook" the books; they falsified the existence of companies owned by Enron. These false companies were given exotic names such as Jedi, Raptor, BLANK, BLANK, and BLANK. California was chosen by Enron leaders to create an energy corridor that could be manipulated to raise the cost of energy. Tim Belden ran the West Coast power grid.

The Enron leaders' idea was to cut off the energy supply until negotiations could be brought about to increase the price of electricity in the state. This caused catastrophic issues such as fires and power shortages. Havoc resulted from these behaviors within the state of California. The consequences of these happenings resulted in expressions such as "Burn, Baby, Burn," made by the Enron leaders who were responsible for the happenings.

Enron leaders lobbied for Congress to pass deregulation of energy laws. These laws were supposed to create competition among energy companies.

California was chosen by Enron to be one of the largest settings for the corporation's illicit operations. There was no limit to how far the people in charge would go to put money in their own bank accounts.

Several top political leaders in the nation were associated with Enron leaders at this time. Perhaps these political leaders were convinced by Enron leaders of the innocence and sincerity of the Enron scheme. A Hollywood movie actor was involved. Ken Lay died of a heart attack before he served any time in prison for his part in the fraud.

Andrew Fastow was asked the question, "Is Enron stock overpriced?" For sixteen years, Arthur Andersen, L.L.C. (Limited Liability Company) served as Enron's auditor. Andersen was one of the "Big Five" accounting firms in existence. Charges of illegal practices were filed in a Texas Court of Law against Arthur Andersen Accounting L.L.C.

Court documents provided truth that Enron and Arthur Andersen had falsely arranged information to indicate millions of dollars of increases in shareholders' equity. Money was taken from Enron and deposited in the bank accounts of the perpetrators of the fraud. The courts of law mandated the dissolution of Arthur Andersen. Enron filed bankruptcy papers.

Enron claimed revenues of nearly $101 billion during the year 2000. The energy company was named by Fortune magazine as "America's Most Innovative Company" for six consecutive years. After court convictions of fraud, many executives were sentenced to prison. Jeffrey Skilling was sentenced to 24 years in prison but, after appeals, served only 12 years.

Andrew Fastow was sentenced to serve six years in a federal prison but served only five years.

Sherron Watkins, a vice president of Enron, was considered the "whistle-blower" of Enron's fraudulent activities. Watkins alerted CEO Ken Lay of accounting irregularities at Enron. She was called to testify before committees of the U.S. House of Representatives. Watkins was recognized in the year 2002 as "Person of The Year" by Time magazine.

Many of the officers of Enron Energy Corporation and leaders of its fake subsidiaries were aware of the fraudulent activities. Some of these leaders received millions of dollars for their participation in the scam. The Enron scam is considered one of the worst in history. It definitely represents the "dark side" of mankind's behavior.

Chapter Thirty-Eight:
The Propitiation of America

"And he himself is the propitiation of our sins, and not for our sins only but also for the whole world."

(I John 2:2)

Propitiation is the act of appeasing God in order to bring about reconciliation. When we sin, we disobey God, who commanded us not to sin. Sin not only hurts the one we have wronged, but also causes damage to ourselves. Does God's holiness demand punishment for the sinner?

Out of love for His earthly children, God sacrificed His only begotten Son, Jesus, on the cross to pay for the debt of the sinner. This had to be immensely painful. Having lost two children, I have personal experience in this heart-rending loss. The excruciating pain associated with the death of a child is beyond description. The death of a child creates a void that can never be filled. It creates a hole in the heart.

Propitiation means satisfaction. Because God loves mankind, He set up the means for salvation and an eternal home for His children. Peace for man lies in propitiation. God Himself came down from heaven and allowed the crucifixion at Golgotha to happen, thus paying for the sins of mankind. This act avoided Divine retribution.

Early offerings found in Scripture for sin included an offering of a blood sacrifice. Without such a sacrifice, there was no remission of sin. Realizing that sin had been committed and anxious for pardon, man brought sacrificial offerings to be placed on the altar before God. This was according to God's instructions in the Old Testament. The sacrifice was to be without blemish.

The belief was that the sacrificial offering was the "scapegoat" for the sin, that was to be burned on the altar – to atone for the sins of the person seeking pardon so that he or she would be forgiven. Explicit directions are given in Scripture that spell out this process. The belief was that, without sacrifice, there is no satisfaction, and without satisfaction, there is no pardon. During this process, the priest was to put his hand upon the sin offering.

The sin was then transferred to the lamb, goat, pigeon, grain, or whatever was being sacrificed. This entire sacrifice was to be consumed with fire. Is it possible that Scripture foretells the end of the world? Will there be another "sacrificial lamb" consumed by fire?

Jesus was the scapegoat who willingly allowed Himself to be nailed to the cross on Calvary to die for our sins. That was the greatest gift of grace that anyone has ever given. The pierced hands and crown of thorns placed on the head of Jesus represent the greatest gift – Himself – that could be given to anyone who asks for it. This present is a large box filled with love and wrapped in grace. And everyone who believes in God's message of salvation receives this gift.

Chapter Thirty-Nine:
The Atonement of America

"God presented him (Jesus) as a sacrifice of atonement, through faith in his blood."

(Romans 3:25)

The definition of atonement is: the reparation for a wrong or injury.

It is one of the themes of the New Testament of the Holy Bible. Atonement is a reference to the purpose for the sacrifice of Jesus. His crucifixion on the cross at Calvary was made in order to reconcile sinners to God. Although the crucifixion of Christ is a New Testament event, "atonement" is an Old Testament term.

Atonement is an action of God. The word can be written in such a way as to emphasize the significance of the meaning: AT - ONE - MENT. A pastor or priest can make atonement for an individual if he/she sins unintentionally. The sinner can also come before God in prayer and ask for forgiveness. God welcomes this action to repair the broken relationship between the sinner and Himself.

The mending action of atonement can be demonstrated by a father's love, which softens the heart of his children and brings about repentance. In Judaism, atonement is known as Yom Kippur. It is the day that means, "We are reconciled with God." Kippur is a Hebrew word that means "to cover," as in "coat with pitch." It also means "to purge."

Atonement is the reuniting of two parties who are at odds with one another. Yom Kippur is the most important holiday (holy day) in the Jewish Faith. It marks the culmination of ten days of awe. It is a time of introspection and repentance.

This important day, often observed by many who do not always attend other Jewish holy days, follows Rosh Hashanah, the Jewish New Year. Attendance at the synagogue increases significantly on this holy day. This is like the spike in attendance in Christian churches at Easter. The holiday is observed by spending the eve of Yom Kippur, as well as the entire following day, in meditation and prayer. It occurs on the tenth day of the seventh month, Tishrei, and is known as the "Sabbath of Sabbaths."

The Jewish calendar is lunar, while the Gregorian calendar used by most of the Western world is solar. This makes the Jewish calendar about ten days short of a solar year. This means that seven years in nineteen have an extra month on the Jewish calendar. This occurrence ensures that Jewish feast days keep to their correct seasons.

The Hebrew word "kaphar" was the protective coating, like pitch, with which the Ark was covered. To "atone" is to make amends.

According to Leviticus 23: 27-30:

"The Lord said to Moses, 'The tenth day of this seventh month is the Day of Atonement. Hold a sacred assembly and deny yourselves, and present an offering made to the Lord by fire. Do no work on that day, because it is the Day of Atonement, when atonement is made for you before your God "

Chapter Forty:
Will God Forgive America?

"Hear their prayer and their plea and uphold their cause. And forgive your people who have sinned against you."

(I Kings 8:50)

Possibly one of the most difficult actions that we find ourselves having to perform is that of forgiving someone for an offense he or she initiated. Offense is a form of the craftiness of Satan, the Father of Lies and ruler of the Worldly Kingdom. It is through offense that discord, disharmony, hatred, and division are culminated. If forgiveness is not given, grievous consequences may follow.

The remnant of the world will be forgiven. The remnant is in this world, but not of this world, and they will be forgiven. The remnant, as stated by Paul in Romans 9:27,

"Though the number of Israelites be like the sand by the sea, only the remnant will be saved."

God provided salvation by sacrificing His Son on the cross at Golgotha, and all—Jew or Gentile, Black or White, rich or poor, male or female—will be forgiven if they seek forgiveness and follow the will of God.

Abba, the Father who loves us, gave us many promises of His faithfulness to guide us to do His will. We are reconciled with God through prayer, repentance, fasting, and adherence to God's Holy Commandments. This is what it takes to heal our land. God blessed this nation from sea to shining sea. But He demands adherence to His Holy Laws.

"Forgive us our trespasses as we forgive those who trespass against us" is easily recognized as the way Jesus taught us to pray in "The Lord's Prayer." We are obliged to forgive others if we expect to be forgiven by the Lord. There is no negotiating with that commandment. We are compelled to honor that decree given by our Sovereign Lord.

I am reminded of the animosity I felt for someone who grievously hurt me after I had done many favors for her. God put it in my mind one day, as I was feeling resentment toward that person, "How dare you not forgive her." We can get our "act together," and by the grace of God, if we focus on the Lord's Word, we will have His power to live a holy existence. We will, at times, be tested by the Lord. We will often be tempted by Satan. At times, we will be misunderstood by those around us.

There may be circumstances where we are ostracized for our spiritual beliefs, but we must remain faithful to the Lord. He will be with us at all times. The following Psalm 23:1-6 is a favorite of many:

"The Lord is my shepherd, I shall not be in want. He makes me lie down in green pastures, He leads me beside quiet waters, He restores my soul. He guides me in paths of righteousness in his name's sake. Even though I

walk through the valley of the shadow of death, I will fear no evil, for you
are with me; your rod and your staff, they comfort me. You prepare a
table before me in the presence of my enemies. You anoint my head with
oil, my cup overflows. Surely goodness and love will follow me All the
days of my life, and I will dwell in The house of the Lord forever."

Chapter Forty-One:
Gettin' Right with God

"God will be with you wherever you go."

(Joshua 1:9)

There is no greater joy in life than to be right with God. We experience an overwhelming peace when we are right with the Lord. Sin separates us from God. When we are not right with God, we experience a gnawing that eats at our insides until we reconcile with our Creator and make restitution for our wrongdoing.

The process of "getting right with God" is dependent upon total sincerity of the deed. It cannot be an action of the moment but must be for the present and all future times. There is no negotiating allowed on this required commitment. The Holy Spirit will not let us have a moment of rest until we are right with "Our Father in Heaven."

This is among the many aspects involved in the Holy Spirit's "job description duties." And He is very trustworthy to carry out His duties. The Holy Spirit is willing to talk the matter over with us in prayer. He will advise us to ask God's Son, Jesus, to soften our hardened hearts.

Remember, the Holy Spirit is the third person of the Holy Trinity that constitutes: God—the Father; Jesus, God—the Son; and God—the Holy

Spirit. Having confessed our sins and asked for forgiveness, we must make restitution to the person or persons we have offended by our sinful behavior. Scripture informs us that we must not only restore, measure for measure, but add a fifth more to the value of what the transgression cost those we offended. God insists that we do it His way if we want the joy and peace He has promised us.

When we sincerely commit our will to do His will, we will expel a great sigh of relief, and a sense of peace will flush through our entire being. We will experience no resentments. We will be content in everything we do. We will be right with the Lord!

After we make peace with the Lord, we are ready to receive the promises God has sent us through the prophets of the Old Testament. We then learn of the wonders of the promises that we are given through His Son in the New Testament. These promises will equip us to cope during hard times. We will be able to turn away from sin and be victorious through Christ.

We will become a new person as each of us makes Christ Lord of our life. As this "born again" person, we will be able to carry the message of salvation to others. Once saved, we will be taught by God's Holy Spirit as we grow in sanctification—the journey of the new Christian and the nominal Christian to be transformed into a mature disciple. This "born again" person evolves into an ambassador of God who characterizes the righteousness of Christ.

Every thought and every behavior will be guided by the Word of God and the example of His Son. There is not one behavior of human beings that has not been addressed in Scripture as acceptable or unacceptable to the Father of Mankind. Our Father is a loving Father who exemplifies the fruit of the Spirit—love, joy, peace, patience, kindness, and understanding. These are the characteristics of the Father and the Son. These characteristics should be found in the born-again believer.

Jesus states in the verses of John 14:7,

"If you know me, you will know my Father as well. From now on, you do know him and have seen him."

People will see the Christ in us. When this phenomenon becomes a reality, we will then know we are fulfilling God's purpose for our lives.

The moment when we realize that we are living our lives by carrying out the business of our Father in heaven will be one of the greatest moments in our lives. This provides the peace that will make loneliness, pain, injustice, and sorrows bearable. This is another grace-gift from God. This endeavor rates high on the scale of fulfillment in the pursuit of happiness.

It is the look we hope to see on the face of our loved ones when we view the body for the last time at a memorial service. This gives us the assurance that is suggested in the song "All is Well with My Soul." When that time draws near in our lives and we are in "God's waiting room," we hope to "rest in peace." "The next stop for us is an eternity spent in heaven with our Abba."

As I finish this book, I want to cover the requirements for salvation in the Judeo-Christian faith: (1) You must believe in God; (2) You must believe Jesus is the Son of God; (3) You must believe Jesus died on the cross to pay the debt for our sins and that He is the Gracegate through which we reach God; and (4) You must believe Jesus arose from the dead on the third day after He was crucified.

This author fears that the people who make up the citizenry of this great nation are abandoning the principles of the Founding Fathers who found favor with the God in whom they professed to believe. I plead with you, dear reader, to turn to God for forgiveness of your sins and for guidance. Please pray for the greatest Spiritual Awakening this world has ever experienced.

God is beckoning me to share my experiences as an ambassador of Christ to help communicate His saving grace. It is my hope and prayer that the Words of Scripture that I share with others will take wings and find a place in their hearts. May God Bless America!

www.ingramcontent.com/pod-product-compliance
Lightning Source LLC
Chambersburg PA
CBHW051137120626
46547CB00012B/838